Day-by-Day Math Thinking Routines in Kindergarten

Day-by-Day Math Thinking Routines in Kindergarten helps you provide students with a review of the foundational ideas in math, every day of the week! Based on the bestselling *Daily Math Thinking Routines in Action*, the book follows the simple premise that frequent, rigorous, engaging practice leads to mastery and retention of concepts, ideas, and skills. These worksheet-free, academically rigorous routines and prompts follow the kindergarten priority standards and include whole group, individual, and partner work. The book can be used with any math program, or for small groups, workstations, or homework.

Inside you will find:

♦ 40 weeks of practice
♦ 1 activity a day
♦ 200 activities total
♦ Answer Key

For each week, the Anchor Routines cover these key areas: Monday: General Thinking Routines; Tuesday: Vocabulary; Wednesday: Place Value; Thursday: Fluency; and Friday: Problem Solving. Get your students' math muscles moving with the easy-to-follow routines in this book!

Dr. Nicki Newton has been an educator for 30 years, working both nationally and internationally with students of all ages. She has worked on developing Math Workshop and Guided Math Institutes around the country; visit her website at www.drnickinewton.com. She is also an avid blogger (www.guidedmath.wordpress.com), tweeter (@drnickimath) and Pinterest pinner (www.pinterest.com/drnicki7).

T0383514

Day-by-Day Math Thinking Routines in Kindergarten

40 Weeks of Quick Prompts and Activities

Dr. Nicki Newton

Routledge
Taylor & Francis Group

NEW YORK AND LONDON

First published 2020
by Routledge
52 Vanderbilt Avenue, New York, NY 10017

and by Routledge
2 Park Square, Milton Park, Abingdon, Oxon, OX14 4RN

Routledge is an imprint of the Taylor & Francis Group, an informa business

Library of Congress Cataloging-in-Publication Data
Names: Newton, Nicki, author.
Title: Day-by-day math thinking routines in kindergarten : 40 weeks of
   quick prompts and activities / Dr. Nicki Newton.
Description: New York, NY : Routledge, 2020.
Identifiers: LCCN 2019036221 (print) | LCCN 2019036222 (ebook) |
   ISBN 9780367421212 (hardback) | ISBN 9780367421205 (paperback) |
   ISBN 9780367821937 (ebook)
Subjects: LCSH: Mathematics—Study and teaching (Kindergarten)—Activity
   programs.
Classification: LCC QA135.6 .N4846 2020 (print) | LCC QA135.6 (ebook) |
   DDC 372.7/044—dc23
LC record available at https://lccn.loc.gov/2019036221
LC ebook record available at https://lccn.loc.gov/2019036222

ISBN: 978-0-367-42121-2 (hbk)
ISBN: 978-0-367-42120-5 (pbk)
ISBN: 978-0-367-82193-7 (ebk)

Typeset in Palatino
by Swales & Willis, Exeter, Devon, UK

Contents

Meet the Author

Dr. Nicki Newton has been an educator for 30 years, working both nationally and internationally, with students of all ages. Having spent the first part of her career as a literacy and social studies specialist, she built on those frameworks to inform her math work. She believes that math is intricately intertwined with reading, writing, listening and speaking. She has worked on developing Math Workshop and Guided Math Institutes around the country. Most recently, she has been helping districts and schools nationwide to integrate their State Standards for Mathematics and think deeply about how to teach these within a Math Workshop model. Dr. Nicki works with teachers, coaches and administrators to make math come alive by considering the powerful impact of building a community of mathematicians who make meaning of real math together. When students do real math, they learn it. They own it, they understand it, and they can do it. Every one of them. Dr. Nicki is also an avid blogger (www.guidedmath.wordpress.com) and Pinterest pinner (https://www.pinterest.com/drnicki7/).

Introduction

Welcome to this exciting new series of daily math thinking routines. I have been doing thinking routines for years. People ask me all the time if I have these written down somewhere. So, I wrote a book. Now, that has turned into a grade level series so that people can do them with prompts that address their grade level standards. This is the anti-worksheet workbook!

The goal is to get students reflecting on their thinking and communicating their mathematical thinking with partners and the whole class about the math they are learning. Marzano (2007)[1] notes that

> initial understanding, albeit a good one, does not suffice for learning that is aimed at long-term retention and use of knowledge. Rather, students must have opportunities to practice new skills and deepen their understanding of new information. Without this type of extended processing, knowledge that students initially understand might fade and be lost over time.

The daily math thinking routines in this book focus on taking Depth of Knowledge activity level 1 activities, to DOK level 2 and 3 activities. Many of the questions are open. For example, we turn the traditional fluency question on its head. Instead of asking students 'What is the answer to 10 − 8?', We ask students to tell us a word problem where the answer is 2. Inspired by Marion Small (2009)[2] we don't just ask what comes after 5, we ask, what is a number that is near 5? What is a number that is far from 5?

In this series, we work mainly work on priority standards, although we do address some of the supporting and additional standards. This book is not intended to cover every standard. Rather it is meant to provide ongoing daily review of the foundational ideas in math. There is a focus for each day of the week.

- Monday: General Thinking Routines
- Tuesday: Vocabulary
- Wednesday: Place Value
- Thursday: Fluency (American and British Number Talks, Number Strings)
- Friday: Problem Solving

There are general daily thinking routines (What Doesn't Belong?, True or False?, Convince Me!), that review various priority standards from the different domains (Geometry, Algebraic Thinking, Counting, Measurement, Number Sense). Every Tuesday there is an emphasis on Vocabulary because math is a language and if you don't know the words then you can't speak it. There is a continuous review of foundational words through different games (Match, Bingo), because students need at least 6 encounters with a word to own it. On Wednesday there is often an emphasis on Place Value. Thursday is always some sort of fluency routine (American or British Number Talks and Number Strings). Finally, Fridays are Problem-Solving routines.

The book starts with a review of prekindergarten standards and then as the weeks progress the current grade level standards are integrated throughout. There is a heavy emphasis on

---

1 Marzano, R. J. (2007). *The art and science of teaching: A comprehensive framework for effective instruction.* ASCD: Virginia.
2 Small, M. (2009). *Good Questions: Great ways to differentiate mathematics instruction.* Teachers College Press: New York.

counting and cardinality and algebraic thinking. There is also an emphasis on geometry concepts and some data and measurement. The word problem types for kindergarten have been woven throughout the year.

Throughout the book there is an emphasis on the mathematical practices/processes (SMP, 2010[3]; NCTM, 2000[4]). Students are expected to problem solve in different ways. They are expected to reason by contextualizing and decontextualizing numbers. They are expected to communicate their thinking to partners and the whole group using the precise mathematical vocabulary. Part of this is reading the work of others, listening to others explanations, writing about their work and then speaking about their work and the work of others in respectful ways. Students are expected to model their thinking with tools and templates. Students are continuously asked to think about the pattern and structure of numbers as they work through the activities.

These activities focus on building mathematical proficiency as defined by the NAP 2001[5]. These activities focus on conceptual understanding, procedural fluency, adaptive reasoning, strategic competence and a student's mathematical disposition. This book can be used with any math program. These are jump starters to the day. They are getting the math muscle moving at the beginning of the day.

Math routines are a form of "guided practice." Marzano (2007) notes that although the:

> guided practice is the place where students—working alone, with other students, or with the teacher—engage in the cognitive processing activities of organizing, reviewing, rehearsing, summarizing, comparing, and contrasting. However, it is important that all students engage in these activities. (Rosenshine, p.7 cited in Marzano, 2007)

These are engaging, standards-based, academically rigorous activities that provide meaningful routines that develop mathematical proficiency. The work can also be used for practice with in small groups, workstations and also sent home as questions for homework.

We have focused on coherence from grade to grade, rigor of thinking, and focus on understanding and being able to explain the math the students are doing. We have intended to take deeper dives into the math, not rushing to the topics of the next grade but going deeper into the topics of the grade at hand (see Figures 1.1–1.4). Here is our criteria for selecting the routines:

♦ Engaging
♦ Easy to learn
♦ Repeatable
♦ Open-ended
♦ Easy to differentiate (adapt and extend for different levels).

3 The Standards of Mathematical Practice. "Common Core State Standards for Mathematical Practice." Washington, D.C.: National Governors Association Center for Best Practices, Council of Chief State School Officers, 2010. Retrieved on December 1, 2019 from: www.corestandards.org/Math/Practice.
4 National Council of Teachers of Mathematics. (2000). *Principles and standards for school mathematics*. Reston, VA: National Council of Teachers of Mathematics.
5 Kilpatrick, J., Swafford, J., and Findell, B. (eds.) (2001). *Adding it up: Helping children learn mathematics*. Washington, DC: National Academy Press.

Figure 1.1 Talking about the Routine!

Week 1 Activities

Monday: What Doesn't Belong?

Look at the different sets. In each set, decide which thing does not belong. Explain why.

2	4
A	1

Tuesday: Alike and Different

How are these shapes alike and different?

Wednesday: Number of the Day

Fill in the boxes based on the number 5.

5

Picture	Ten Frame

Number Path				
1	2	3	4	5

Thursday: Number Talk

- Show 3 on your fingers.
- Show 3 fingers in a different way.
- Show 3 in a different way.

Friday: Make Your Own Problem

There were 3 giraffes and 1 more came. How many are there?

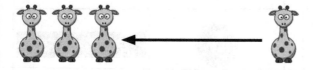

Figure 1.2 The Math Routine Cycle of Engagement

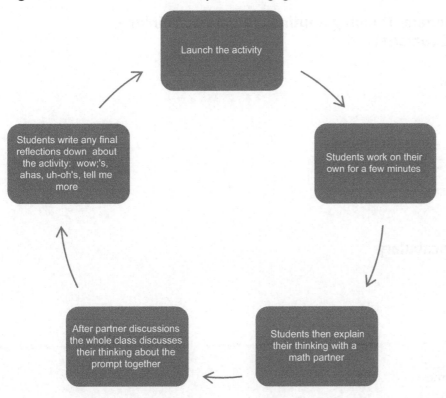

Step 1: Students are given the launch prompt. The teacher explains the prompt and makes sure that everyone understands what they are working on.

Step 2: They are given a few minutes to work on that prompt by themselves.

Step 3: The next step is for students to work with a math partner. As they work with this partner, students are expected to listen to what their partner did as well as explain their own work.

Step 4: Students come back together as a whole group and discuss the math. They are encouraged to talk about how they solved it and the similarities and differences between their thinking and their partner's thinking.

Step 5: Students reflect on the prompt of the day, thinking about what wowed them, what made them say ah-ha, what made them say uh-oh, what made them say, "I need to know more about this."

Thinking Activities

These are carefully planned practice activities to get students to think. They are **not meant to be used as a workbook**. This is a thinking activity book. The emphasis is on students doing their own work, explaining what they did with a partner and then sharing out to the entire class.

Overview of the Routines

Monday Routines – General Thinking Routines (Algebraic Thinking, Measurement, Data, Geometry)

- Convince Me!
- Counting Arrangements
- Counting Jars
- Counting Fingers
- Find and Fix the Error
- Legs and Feet
- Reasoning Matrices
- True or False
- 2 Arguments
- What Doesn't Belong?

Tuesday Routines – Vocabulary

- Alike and Different
- Before and After
- Counting Words
- Frayer Model
- It Is/It Isn't
- Draw and Discuss
- More, Fewer, or the Same
- Vocabulary Brainstorm

Wednesday Routines – Place Value

- Composing and Decomposing Numbers
- More, Fewer, or the Same
- Find and Fix the Error
- Greater Than, Less Than, in Between
- Guess My Number
- How Many More to
- Number Bond It!
- Number Scramble
- Number of the Day
- Positional Words

Thursday Routines – Number Talks

- Number Talks
- Number Strings

Friday Routines – Problem Solving

- Equation Match
- Make Your Own Problem
- Match the Model
- Model It!
- What's the Problem?
- What's the Story?
- What's the Question? (3 Read Protocol)

Figure 1.3 Overview of the Routines

Routine	Purpose	Description
Before and After	This routine focuses on the skills of naming the numbers before and after each other.	Students are given numbers and they have to name the number before and/or the number after.
Composing Numbers	Composing and decomposing numbers is a stepping stone to adding and subtracting.	Students use 10 frames to compose and decompose different numbers.
Convince Me!	This routine focuses on students reasoning about different topics. They have to convince their peers about specific statements.	Students are given different things to think about like statements or equations and they have to convince their peers that they are correct.
Counting Fingers	Fingers are so important in developing number sense. This routine focuses on counting finger representations and discussing how they are alike and different.	Students look at and discuss the finger representations. They discuss which one is more, how many more, what is the same about the representations and what is different.
Counting Jar	This routine focuses on making reasonable estimates of quantities.	Students are shown a counting jar with a specific amount of items. They have to make a reasonable estimate and then one of the students leads the count to determine the exact amount. Students then discuss what is a close estimate and what is one that is a high or low estimate.
Counting Arrangements	This routine focuses on counting objects in various arrangements – line, array, circle and scattered.	Students are shown a variety of counting cards and they must count the objects in different arrangements. Some of these cards work on counting in different arrangements and others work on the idea of conservation – the idea that no matter what the arrangement, the amount stays the same.
Equation Match	This routine focuses on students thinking about which operation they would use to solve a problem. It requires that they reason about the actions that are happening in the problem and then what they are required to do to solve the problem.	Students are trying to match the word problem and the equation.

Routine	Purpose	Description
Find and Fix the Error	This routine requires that students analyze the work of others and discuss what went well or what went wrong. The purpose of the routine is not only to get students to identify common errors but also to get them to justify their own thinking about the problem.	Students think about a problem either by themselves, with a partner or with the whole group that is either done correctly or incorrectly. They have to figure out why it is done incorrectly or correctly and discuss.
Frayer Model	This routine is meant to get students talking about concepts. They are supposed to talk about the definition, what happens in real life, sketch an example and also give non-examples.	Students are given a template with labels. They work through the template writing and drawing about the specified topic.
Guess My Number	This routine gives students a variety of clues about a number and asks the students to guess which number it might be given all the clues. Students have to use their understanding of place value and math vocabulary to figure out which number is being discussed.	In this routine, students are given various clues about a number and they must use the clues to guess which number it is.
How Many More to	In this routine, students are asked to tell how many to a specific number. Again, this is another place value routine, asking students to reason about numbers on the number line.	In this routine, students are given a specific number and they have to tell how many more to the target number.
It Is/It Isn't	This routine can be used in a variety of ways. Students have to look at the topic and decide what it is and what it isn't. It is another way of looking at example, non-example.	In this routine, students discuss what something is and what it isn't.
Legs and Feet	Legs and Feet is a great arithmetic routine which gets students to use various operations to figure out how many animals there are by working with numbers.	Students look at different animals and think about how many legs and feet there could be given that number of animals.
Make Your Own Problem	In this word problem routine students get to pick their own numbers to create and then solve a word problem.	Students fill in the blanks with numbers to make their own problems.
Match the Model	In this word problem routine, students have to find the word problem that matches the model. It is another way to work on representation of word problems.	Students are trying to pair the word problem and the model.

Routine	Purpose	Description
Model It!	In this word problem routine, students are focusing on representing word problems in a variety of ways.	Students have to represent their thinking about a word problem with various models.
More, Fewer, or the Same	In this place value routine, students are comparing quantities and describing them with the terms, more, fewer, or the same.	Students look at pictures of various items and describe them in relationship to each other.
Number Bond It!	In this routine, students are working on decomposing numbers in a variety of ways.	Students use number bonds to break apart numbers in different ways.
Number of the Day	This activity focuses on students modeling numbers in a variety of ways.	This activity has a given number and students have to represent that number in different ways.
Number Scramble	This activity focuses on sequencing numbers correctly.	Students have to put numbers in the correct sequence on the number path.
Number Talk	This activity focuses on number sense. Students compose and decompose numbers as well as add and subtract numbers.	There are a few different ways that students do this activity. One approach involves the teacher working with the students on showing a number in a variety of ways. Another activity is that the teacher gives the students number strings around a specific concept. For example subtracting 1 from a number and students work those problems and discuss the strategy.
Number Strings	In this routine, students are looking at the relationship between the numbers in the string.	Students work out the different problems and discuss the various strategies they are using.
Number Scramble	Students should understand, know and recognize the counting sequence to 20.	In this routine students have to order the numbers on the number path.
Reasoning Matrices	Reasoning matrices helps students to reason about information and decide what makes sense given that information.	In this routine, students are given information about children and they have to decide which information matches which child.
Reasoning	Students should be able to listen to information and then make decision s based on that information.	Students compare objects or numbers and talk about their relationships.

Routine	Purpose	Description
True or False?	This activity focuses on students reasoning about what is true or false.	Students are given different things to think about like statements about shapes or equations and they have to state and prove whether they are true or false.
2 Arguments	In this reasoning routine, students are thinking about common errors that students make when doing various math tasks like missing numbers, working with properties and working with the equal sign.	Students listen to the way 2 different students approached a problem, decide who they agreed with and defend their thinking.
Counting Words	This activity focuses on counting words.	Students count to a particular number.
More, Fewer, or the Same	This activity focuses on developing an understanding of more, fewer, and the same.	Students are shown a picture and they have to discuss what is more, fewer, or the same in the picture.
Greater Than, Less Than, in Between	Students should understand the relationship of numbers to each other on the number line	Students have to discuss number relationships given specific numbers.
Positional Words	This activity focuses on learning positional words.	Students are given specific instructions on where to place an object so that they learn the positional words.
Alike and Different	This activity focuses on students reasoning about what is the same and what is different with objects.	Students are shown 2 or 3 different things and they have to discuss how they are alike and different.
Draw and Discuss	Students should be able to discuss 2D shapes.	In this routine students draw and discuss different 2D shapes.
What Doesn't Belong?	This is a reasoning activity where students have to choose which objects they can group together and why. The emphasis is on justification.	Students have 4 squares. They have to figure out which object does not belong.
What's the Story?	Students should be able to tell a story when given objects or a picture.	In this routine, students are shown a picture and they have to tell what is happening in the story.
What's the Question?	Students should be able to reason about a story context.	Students are given a story context and they have to come up with questions about that context.
Which One Is the Subtraction Problem?	Students should learn the difference between addition and subtraction problems.	Students have to identify subtraction problems.

Questioning Is the Key 🗝

To Unlock the Magic of Thinking, You Need Good Questions!

Figure 1.4

Launch Questions (Before the Activity)	Process Questions (During the Activity)
◆ What is this prompt asking us to do? ◆ How will you start? ◆ What are you thinking? ◆ Explain to your math partner, your understanding of the question. ◆ What will you do to solve this problem?	◆ What will you do first? ◆ How will you organize your thinking? ◆ What might you do to get started? ◆ What is your strategy? ◆ Why did you….? ◆ Why are you doing that? ◆ Is that working? Does it make sense? ◆ Is that a reasonable answer? ◆ Can you prove it? ◆ Are you sure about that answer? ◆ How do you know you are correct?
Debrief Questions (After the Activity)	**Partner Questions (Guide Student Conversations)**
◆ What did you do? ◆ How did you get your answer? ◆ How do you know it is correct? ◆ Can you prove it? ◆ Convince me that you have the correct answer ◆ Is there another way to think about this problem?	◆ Tell me what you did. ◆ Tell me more about your model. ◆ Tell me more about your drawing. ◆ Tell me more about your calculations. ◆ Tell me more about your thinking. ◆ Can you prove it? ◆ How do you know you are right? ◆ I understand what you did. ◆ I don't understand what you did yet.

Daily Routines

Week 1 Teacher Notes

Monday: What Doesn't Belong?

In this routine students have to discuss what 3 of the following numbers, letters, shapes and images belong. They should be able to talk about the difference between numbers and letters. You could extend the discussion by asking students to name more letters and more numbers. The students should be able to talk about why the giraffe does not belong.

Tuesday: Alike and Different

Students should be able to discuss how the shapes are alike with sides that are closed how they have points (vertices) and how the sides are straight. We want to focus on the attributes of the shapes.

Wednesday: Number of the Day

This is an opportunity for students to work with numbers and their representations. They draw them and also put them on the 10 frame. They circle it on the number path.

Thursday: Number Talk

This is an opportunity for students to work with composing and decomposing numbers.

Friday: What's the Story?

You want students to act this out and then discuss the pictures.

Monday: What Doesn't Belong?

Look at the different sets. In each set, decide which thing does not belong. Explain why.

A.

3	5
A	1

B.

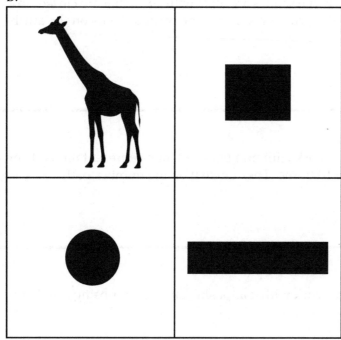

Tuesday: Alike and Different

Discuss how the shapes are alike and different with your partner and then the class.

Wednesday: Number of the Day

Look at the number of the day. Fill in the spaces using that number.

3

Draw 3 things.	Represent the number 3 in the 10 frame.

Number path

1	2	3	4	5

Thursday: Number Talk

Show 3 on your fingers.
Show 3 fingers in a different way.
Show 3 in a different way.

Friday: What's the Story?

Look at the picture. Tell a story about the picture to your partner.

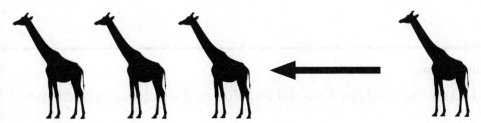

Week 2 Teacher Notes

Monday: What Doesn't Belong?

Here the students will discuss what is the same and what is different in the boxes.

Tuesday: Alike and Different

Students will discuss what is alike and what is different about the shapes.

Wednesday: Number Scramble

Students will talk and order the numbers on the number line.

Thursday: Number Talk

Students work on representing a number on their fingers in different ways.

Friday: Problem Solving

Students would act out the word problems and then discuss the pictorial representation.

Monday: What Doesn't Belong?

Look at the pictures in the set. Decide which one doesn't belong. Explain it to your partner.

A.

B.

Tuesday: Alike and Different

Look at the 2 solids. Talk about what is alike and what is different.

Wednesday: Number Scramble

Circle the number path that is correct. Explain to your partner why it is correct.

A.

1	4	3	2	7

B.

1	2	4	5	3

C.

1	2	3	4	5

Thursday: Number Talk

Show me 4 on your fingers.

Show me 4 on your fingers in a different way?

Friday: Problem Solving

Look at the picture below. Tell a story about that picture.

Week 3 Teacher Notes

Monday: Counting Jar

Teacher prepares a counting jar with 10 items or less. Students work on the counting jar by estimating how many objects are in the jar (in the beginning it should be amounts less than 10). Then, the "Countess" or "Count" leads the count along with the class.

Tuesday: More, Fewer, or the Same

This routine gives students an opportunity to discuss the terms more, fewer or the same.

Wednesday: True or False?

This is a reasoning routine where students have to justify their thinking. Students discuss whether or not this is a circle.

Thursday: Number Talk

Students work on representing a number on their fingers in different ways.

Friday: Problem Solving

Students act out the word problems and then discuss the pictorial representation.

Monday: Counting Jar

First, we are going to estimate – take a thinking guess – of all the bears that are in the guessing jar.

Then, the "Countess" or "Count" is going to count them.

Tuesday: More, Fewer, or the Same

Describe the insects using the words more, fewer and the same.

Wednesday: True or False?

This is a circle. True or false? Explain your thinking.

Thursday: Number Talk

Show me 5 on your fingers.

Show me 5 on your fingers in a different way.

Friday: Problem Solving

Look at the picture. Tell a story about these cows.

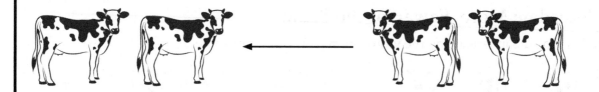

Week 4 Teacher Notes

Monday: Counting Arrangements

Students are focusing on counting in different arrangements.

Tuesday: Positional Words

Students are working on positional words through hands-on activities.

Wednesday: Convince Me!

Students have to reason about numbers. They should use real objects and pictures.

Thursday: Number Talk

Students work on representing numbers with their fingers, pictures and on the number path.

Friday: Problem Solving

Students act out the word problems and then discuss the pictorial representation.

Monday: Counting Arrangements

How many cats are there in each square?

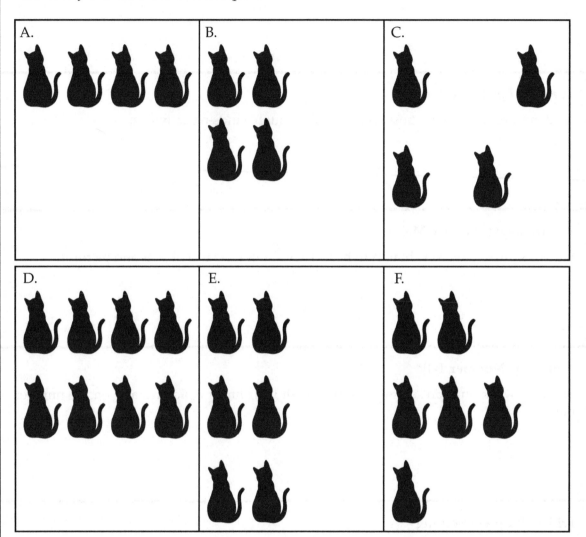

Tuesday: Positional Words

Everybody take your pencil!

Put it on top of your head.
Put it under your chin.
Put it through your fingers.
Put it beside your thumb.

Wednesday: Convince Me!

Use numbers, words, pictures, fingers and five frames to prove this statement.

3 is more than 1.

Thursday: Number Talk

Show 6:

On your fingers in 2 different ways.

With a picture.

Friday: Problem Solving

There were 4 ladybugs and 2 more came. How many are there now?

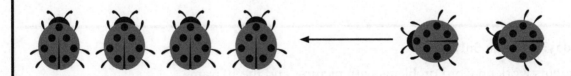

Monday: What Doesn't Belong?

In this routine, students discuss what doesn't belong. They are talking about the difference between 2D shapes and 3D shapes. They are also discussing the difference between numbers and letters.

Tuesday: More, Fewer, or the Same

Students discuss the pictures in relationship to each other. The focus is on understanding the terms of comparison.

Wednesday: Number of the Day

Students represent numbers in a variety of ways.

Thursday: Number Talk

Students work on composing numbers with their fingers.

Friday: Problem Solving

Students work on word problems with pictures and the 10 frame.

Monday: What Doesn't Belong?

Look at the 2 different sets. Decide and discuss what doesn't belong in each set. Explain why to your partner.

A.

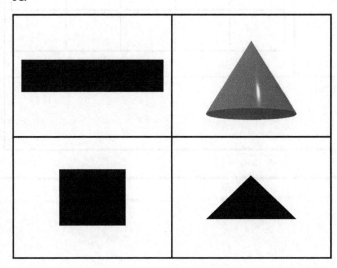

B.

3	2
1	B

Tuesday: More, Fewer, or the Same

Discuss the insects using the words more, fewer and the same.

Wednesday: Number of the Day

Look at the number of the day. Fill in the squares using that number.

4

Write the number.	Represent the number in the ten frame.

Make a picture to represent the number.

Thursday: Number Talk

Show me 7 on your fingers.

Show me 7 in a different way on your fingers.

Friday: Problem Solving

There were 5 ladybugs and 1 more came. How many are there now?

Draw it in the 10 frame.

Monday: Counting Jar

Students work on the counting jar by estimating how many objects are in it (in the beginning it should be amounts less than 10). Then, the "Countess" or "Count" leads the count along with the class.

Tuesday: Positional Words

Students are working on positional words through hands-on activities.

Wednesday: Number of the Day

Students represent numbers in a variety of ways.

Thursday: Number Talk

Students discuss what happens when you add 1 to a number. They should act it out and draw examples as well as explore it on the number line.

Friday: Problem Solving

Students work on word problems with pictures and the 10 frame.

Week 6 Activities

Monday: Counting Jar

First we are going to estimate – take a thinking guess – of all the things that are in the guessing jar.

Then, the "Countess" or "Count" is going to count it.

Tuesday: Positional Words

Everybody take your pencil!

Put it above your head.
Put it below your chin.
Put it behind your ear.
Put it underneath your desk.

Wednesday: Number of the Day

Look at the number of the day. Fill in the squares using that number.

5

Number word	Ten frame
Picture	

Thursday: Number Talk

What happens when we add 1 to a number?

2 + 1
3 + 1
4 + 1
5 + 1

1	2	3	4	5	6	7	8	9	10

Friday: Problem Solving

Tell a story about the dogs. It can be a join story or a take away story.

Monday: Counting Jar

Students work on the counting jar by estimating how many objects are in it (in the beginning it should be amounts less than 10). Then, the "Countess" or "Count" leads the count along with the class.

Tuesday: Positional Words

Students are working on positional words through hands-on activities.

Wednesday: Number of the Day

Students represent numbers in a variety of ways.

Thursday: Number Talk

Students discuss what happens when you take 1 from a number. They should act it out and draw examples as well as explore it on the number line.

Friday: Problem Solving

Students work on word problems with pictures and the 10 frame.

Week 7 Activities

Monday: Counting Jar

The teacher puts 10 or less cubes in a jar and the students have to take a thinking guess of how many there could be. The "Countess" or "Count" then leads the count for the class.

Tuesday: Positional Words

Everybody take your crayon!

Draw a circle.
Put a triangle on top of the circle.
Put a square under the circle.
Add a shape beside the circle.

Wednesday: Number of the Day

Look at the number of the day. Fill in the squares using that number.

6

Number	Ten frame
Picture	

Thursday: Number Talk

What happens when we add 0 to a number? Discuss and explain your thinking with numbers, words and pictures.

Friday: Problem Solving

Look at the picture. Tell a join or a take away story.

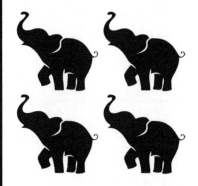

Week 8 Teacher Notes

Monday: Counting Arrangements

Students work on counting the elephants in different arrangements.

Tuesday: Positional Words

Students work on position words by acting them out.

Wednesday: Convince Me!

Students have to reason about their numbers using objects and drawings.

Thursday: Number Talk

Students work on finger representations to compose numbers.

Friday: Problem Solving

Students work on representing word problems in different ways.

Monday: Counting Arrangements

Count the elephants in each box. How many are there?

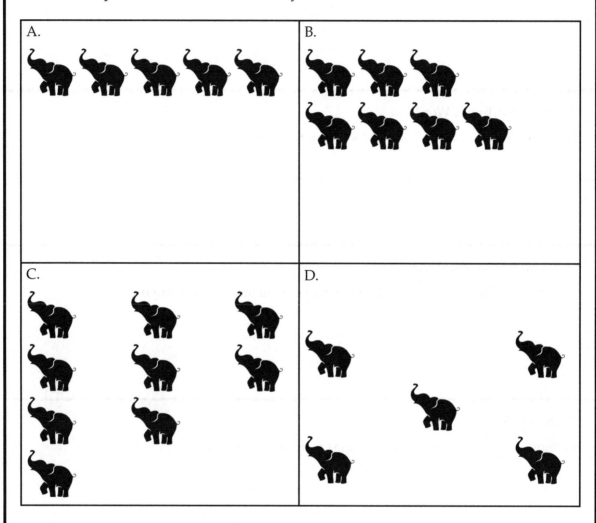

A.

B.

C.

D.

Tuesday: Positional Words

Everybody take your crayon!

Put it underneath your chin.
Put it near the pencil.
Put it beside a book.
Put it in between your thumb and finger.

Wednesday: Convince Me!

Read the statement. Prove it with fingers, counters, 10 frames, number paths and more.

7 is more than 5.

Thursday: Number Talk

Show me 8 on your fingers.

Show me 8 on your fingers in a different way.

Friday: Problem Solving

There was 1 monkey and 3 more came. How many are there now?

Model it on the 10 frame.

Week 9 Teacher Notes

Monday: What Doesn't Belong?

Students reason about what belongs and what doesn't belong in the squares.

Tuesday: Alike and Different

Students have to discuss how the zebra and the monkey are alike and different.

Wednesday: Number of the Day

Students work on the representation of numbers in a variety of ways.

Thursday: Number Talk

Students work on finger representations.

Friday: Problem Solving

Students work on representing word problems in different ways.

Monday: What Doesn't Belong?

Look at the 2 different sets. Figure out what doesn't belong in each set. Discuss it with your partner and then the class. Explain your thinking.

A.

B.

Tuesday: Alike and Different

Look at the 2 animals. Discuss how they are alike and different.

Wednesday: Number of the Day

Look at the number of the day. Fill in the squares using that number.

7

Number	Ten frame

Picture

Thursday: Number Talk

Discuss the number 5. Tell everything you know about it.

Friday: Problem Solving

There were 3 monkeys. Two left. How many are there now?

Model it on the 5 frame.

Answer:

Week 10 Teacher Notes

Monday: Counting Fingers

Students discuss how many by counting and discussing the various finger representations.

Tuesday: Counting Words

Students work on counting to 20.

1	2	3	4	5	6	7	8	9	10	11	12	13	14	15	16	17	18	19	20

Wednesday: Number of the Day

Students work on representing numbers in a variety of ways.

Thursday: Number Talk

Students work on composing and decomposing numbers with their fingers.

Friday: Problem Solving

Students work on representing word problems in a variety of ways.

Monday: Counting Fingers

How many fingers do you see?

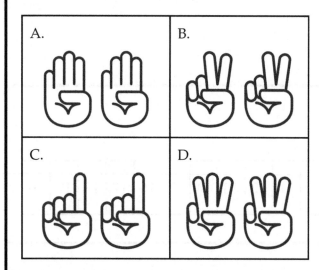

Tuesday: Counting Words

Let's count to 20.

A. What comes before 10?

B. What comes after 15?

C. What comes before 20?

D. You ask a before or after question about the numbers to 20.

1	2	3	4	5	6	7	8	9	10	11	12	13	14	15	16	17	18	19	20

Wednesday: Number of the Day

Look at the number of the day. Fill in the squares using that number.

8

Number	Ten frame
Picture	

Thursday: Number Talk

How can we make 7 on our fingers?

What is another way?

What is another way?

Friday: Problem Solving

There were 4 zebras. Two left. How many are there now?

Model it on the 5 frame.

Answer:

Week 11 Teacher Notes

Monday: Counting Jar

The teacher puts no more than 15 objects in a jar and the students have to take a thinking guess of how many there could be. The "Countess" or "Count" then leads the class in counting the objects.

Tuesday: More, Fewer, or the Same

Students will discuss the fruits using comparison language.

Wednesday: True or False?

Students discuss numbers and prove their thinking using objects and drawings.

Thursday: Number Talk

Students practice composing and decomposing numbers with finger patterns.

Friday: Problem Solving

Students work on problem solving using a variety of tools and models.

Week 11 Activities

Monday: Counting Jar

First, we are going to estimate – take a thinking guess – of all the crayons that are in the guessing jar. Then, the "Countess" or the "Count" will lead us in a count of them.

Tuesday: More, Fewer, or the Same

Look at the fruit. Discuss what you see using the terms "more," "fewer" or "the same as".

Wednesday: True or False?

Discuss the statement. Decide if it is "true" or "false." Defend your thinking with numbers, words and pictures.

2 is more than 3

Thursday: Number Talk

Show me 8 on your fingers.

Show me 8 on your fingers in a different way.

Show me 8 on your fingers in another way.

Friday: Problem Solving

Tell a story about the picture.

Week 12 Teacher Notes

Monday: Counting Arrangements

Students work on counting the objects in different arrangements.

Tuesday: Positional Words

Students work on positional words by acting them out.

Wednesday: Convince Me!

Students discuss numbers in a variety of ways and reason about their relationships.

Thursday: Number Talk

Students work on composing numbers with their fingers.

Friday: Problem Solving

Students work on word problems with a variety of models and tools.

Monday: Counting Arrangements

How many are there in each box?

A.

B.

C.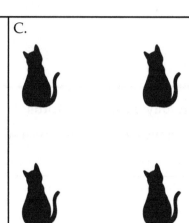

Tuesday: Positional Words

Everybody take your pencil!

Put the pencil beside the crayon.
Put the pencil in between 2 crayons.
Put the pencil on top of a book.
Put the pencil to the right of the book.
Put the pencil underneath the book.

Wednesday: Convince Me!

Look at the statement. Prove that it is true with numbers, words and pictures.

8 is less than 10.

Thursday: Number Talk

How can we make 9?

Show me 9 on your fingers.

Show me 9 on your fingers in a different way.

Show me 9 on your fingers in another way.

Friday: Problem Solving

Read and discuss the problem. Show your thinking on the models below.

There were 2 cows. One left. How many are there now?

Solve it with the picture.	Draw it in the 5 frame.	Solve it on the number path
		1 2 3 4 5

Week 13 Teacher Notes

Monday: What Doesn't Belong?

Students reason about what goes together and what doesn't.

Tuesday: Alike and Different

Students discuss how these animals are the same and different.

Wednesday: Number of the Day

Students work on representing numbers in a variety of ways.

Thursday: Number Talk

Students work on composing numbers with finger combinations.

Friday: Problem Solving

Students work on modeling word problems with different tools.

Monday: What Doesn't Belong?

Look at each set and decide which object doesn't belong. Discuss why.

A.

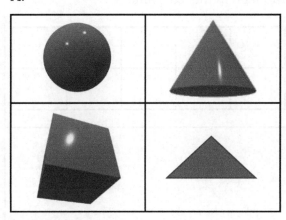

B.

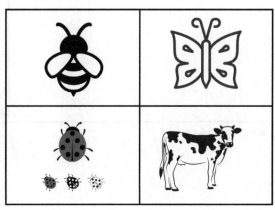

Tuesday: Alike and Different

Look at the 2 pictures. Discuss how they are alike and how they are different.

Wednesday: Number of the Day

Use the number of the day to do the activities in each square.

Look at the number of the day. Fill in the squares using that number.

10

Write the number.	Model it in the ten frame.

Draw 10 things.

Thursday: Number Talk

Show me how to make 10 on your fingers.

Show me another way to make 10 on your fingers.

Friday: Problem Solving

Read the problem. Show your thinking on the models below.

There were 4 butterflies. One left. How many are there now?

Picture	5 Frame	Number Path
		1 2 3 4 5

Week 14 Teacher Notes

Monday: Finger Counting

Students work on counting finger patterns.

Tuesday: Counting Words

Students work on counting words.

Wednesday: Number Bond It!

Students work on decomposing numbers with the number bond.

Thursday: Number Strings

Students should discuss counting on from the big number.

Friday: Problem Solving

Students work on solving word problems with a variety of models.

Monday: Finger Counting.

How many fingers do you see?

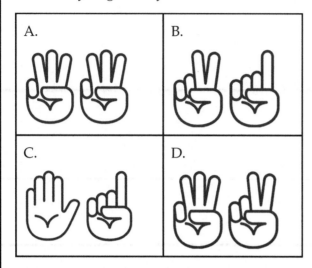

Tuesday: Counting Words

Let's count to 30.
What is the number that comes after 9?
What is the number that comes after 10?
What is the number that comes after 19?
What is the number that comes after 29?

Wednesday: Number Bond It!

Break apart the number 4 in different ways in the number bonds.

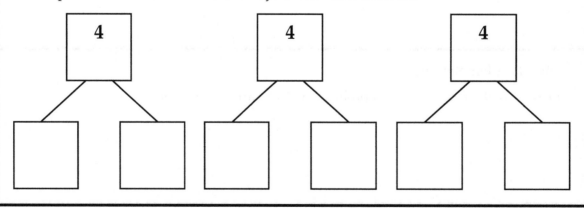

Thursday: Number Strings

What happens when you count on 1 or 2?

2 + 2
1 + 3
4 + 2
1 + 5
7 + 2

1	2	3	4	5	6	7	8	9	10

Friday: Problem Solving

Read the problem. Show your thinking using the models.

There were 3 whales. Three left. How many are there now?

Picture	5 Frame	Number Path
🐋 🐋 🐋		1 2 3 4 5

Week 15 Teacher Notes

Monday: Counting Jar

Students work on estimating and counting markers. The emphasis is on students estimating.

Tuesday: Frayer Model

Students discuss the ideas of numbers and how we use them in real life.

Wednesday: True or False?

Students discuss whether this is a rectangle by thinking and talking about the attributes.

Thursday: Number Talk

Students discuss what happens when we subtract 1 or 2 from a number.

Friday: Problem Solving

Students work on problem solving with a variety of tools.

Week 15 Activities

Monday: Counting Jar

First we are going to estimate – take a thinking guess – of all the things that are in the guessing jar.
Then, the "Count" or "Countess" is going to count them.

Tuesday: Frayer Model

Discuss the word "Numbers" and fill in the boxes to give examples about this word.

Numbers

Example	Where We See Them in Real Life
Our Favorite Numbers	Non-example

Wednesday: True or False?

Look at the statement. Discuss with the class if this is true or false. Explain why.
This is a rectangle!

Thursday: Number Talk

What happens when you take 1 or 2 away from a number?

1 – 1
2 – 2
3 – 1
4 – 2
5 – 1

1	2	3	4	5	6	7	8	9	10

Friday: Problem Solving

Read the story. Show your thinking on the models below.

There were 4 giraffes. One left. How many are there now?

Solve it with the picture.	Draw it in the 5 frame.	Solve it on the number path.
	◯ ◯ ◯ ⬭̸	

1	2	3	4	5

Monday: Counting Arrangements

Students count items in a variety of arrangements.

Tuesday: Vocabulary

Students name some of the shapes that they know.

Wednesday: Convince Me!

Students discuss the relationship between numbers.

Thursday: Number Talk

Students discuss what it means to take a number away from itself.

Friday: Problem Solving

Students work on word problems using a variety of models.

Monday: Counting Arrangements

Count the balls in each set.

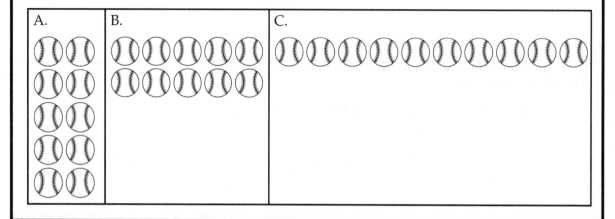

Tuesday: Vocabulary

Name and draw some shapes that you know!

Wednesday: Convince Me!

Convince me that 5 is less than 10. Use numbers, words and pictures to explain your thinking.

Thursday: Number Talk

What happens when you take away a number from itself?

1 − 1
2 − 2
3 − 3
4 − 4
5 − 5

0	1	2	3	4	5

Friday: Problem Solving

Read the problem. Show your thinking on the models below.

There were 5 fish. One left. How many are there now?

Solve it with the picture.	Draw it in the 5 frame.	Solve it on the number path.
	◯ ◯ ◯ ◯ ◯		1	2	3	4	5	

Monday: What Doesn't Belong?

Students reason about addition problems. When I do this with them, I have them think about 1 box at a time. We write the sum in the corner and circle it and then do the next box. At the end, we discuss which one doesn't belong.

Tuesday: Alike and Different

Students work on discussing how the figures are alike and different.

Wednesday: Number of the Day

Students represent numbers in a variety of ways.

Thursday: Number Talk

Students discuss what happens when you take 0 away from a number.

Friday: Problem Solving

Students solve a word problem with different models.

Week 17 Activities

Monday: What Doesn't Belong?

Look at the set of problems. Decide which one does not belong. Explain why.

2 + 1	3 + 0
4 – 1	0 + 2

Tuesday: Alike and Different

Look at the shapes. Discuss what is alike and what is different about them.

Wednesday: Number of the Day

Look at the number. Represent it in different ways in the boxes below.

10

Write the number.	Represent 10 items in the 10 frame.				
Draw a picture with 10 things.					

Thursday: Number Talk

What happens when you take 0 away from a number?

1 − 0
2 − 0
3 − 0
4 − 0
5 − 0

| 0 | 1 | 2 | 3 | 4 | 5 | 6 | 7 | 8 | 9 | 10 |

Friday: Problem Solving

Read the problem. Show your thinking on the models below.

There were 5 ladybugs. Five left. How many are there now?

Picture	5 Frame	Number Path
🐞 🐞 🐞 🐞 🐞		1 2 3 4 5

Week 18 Teacher Notes

Monday: Finger Counting

Students work on counting fingers and discussing quantities.

Tuesday: Before and After

Students work on naming the number before and after.

Wednesday: Number Bond It!

Students work on decomposing a number with number bonds.

Thursday: Number Talk

Students work on adding 2 or 3 to a number. The focus should be on counting on from the larger number.

Friday: Problem Solving

Students work on solving word problems with different models.

Monday: Finger Counting

How many fingers do you see?

A.	B.
C.	D.

Tuesday: Before and After

Name the number before 10.
Name the number after 8.
Name the number before 20.
Name the number after 15.

1	2	3	4	5	6	7	8	9	10	11	12	13	14	15	16	17	18	19	20

Wednesday: Number Bond It!

Show different ways to break apart 6 in the number bonds.

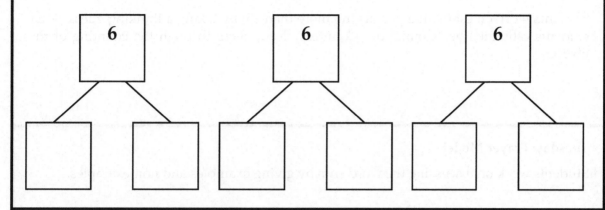

Thursday: Number Talk

What happens when you add 2 or 3 to a number?

1 + 2
2 + 3
3 + 2
4 + 3

0	1	2	3	4	5	6	7	8	9	10

Friday: Problem Solving

Read the problem. Show your thinking in the models below.

There were 4 cats. Two left. How many are there now?

Show with a picture.	Show on the 5 frame.	Show on the number path.
🐈🐈🐈🐈		1 2 3 4 5

Week 19 Teacher Notes

Monday: Counting Jar

Students work on estimating pencils (no more than 15) by taking a thinking guess. After students estimate, the "Count" or "Countess" leads them through the counting of the objects.

Tuesday: Frayer Model

Students work on discussing the word sum by giving examples and non-examples.

Wednesday: True or False?

Students have to reason about an equation.

Thursday: Number Talk

Students work on subtracting 2 from a number using the number path.

Friday: Problem Solving

Students work on solving word problems using a variety of models.

Monday: Counting Jar

First we are going to estimate – take a thinking guess – of all the pencils that are in the guessing jar (no more than 15).

Then, the "Count" or "Countess" is going to count them.

Tuesday: Frayer Model

Discuss the word "sum" in different ways. Use the frayer model as your guide.

Sum

What it means	An example
How we use it in everyday life	Non-example

Wednesday: True or False?

Look at the statement. Decide if it is true or false. Defend your thinking with numbers, words and pictures.

$$2 + 2 = 4$$

Thursday: Number Talk

What happens when you take 2 or 3 from a number?

4 – 2
5 – 3
6 – 2
7 – 3

0	1	2	3	4	5	6	7	8	9	10

Friday: Problem Solving

Read the problem. Show your thinking in the models below.

There were 5 cats and 2 dogs. How many animals are there altogether?

Picture	10 frame	Solve it on the Number Path.
		1 2 3 4 5 6 7 8 9 10

Week 20 Teacher Notes

Monday: Counting Arrangements

Students work on counting objects in different arrangements.

Tuesday: Vocabulary

Students have to name some figures that they know and discuss their attributes.

Wednesday: Convince Me!

Students have to discuss equations and prove their reasoning with pictures.

Thursday: Number Talk

In this number talk students explore taking away a number from 10.

Friday: Problem Solving

Students work on solving word problems with a variety of models.

Monday: Counting Arrangements

Count the penguins in each box.

A.	B.
C.	D.

Tuesday: Vocabulary

Name some number words that you know. Write down the numbers.

Wednesday: Convince Me!

Use words, numbers and pictures to prove that the equation is true.

$$5 - 4 = 1$$

Thursday: Number Talk

What do you think about when you are taking a number away from ten?

10 – 1
10 – 2
10 – 3
10 – 4
10 – 5

1	2	3	4	5	6	7	8	9	10

Friday: Problem Solving

Read the problem. Show your thinking on the models below.

There were 3 cats and 4 dogs. How many animals are there altogether?

Picture	10 frame	Number path to 10

Week 21 Teacher Notes

Monday: What Doesn't Belong?

Students have to select the one that doesn't belong.

Tuesday: Alike and Different

Students have to talk about what is alike and what is different.

Wednesday: Number Bond It!

Students have to decompose 10 in different ways. Answers vary.

Thursday: Number Talk

Students discuss what happens when you subtract 0 from a number.

Friday: Equation Match

Students have to read the problem and then match it with the correct equation.

Monday: What Doesn't Belong?

Look at the set of numbers. Discuss and decide which one doesn't belong and why.

1 + 1	2 + 0
2 – 0	1 + 0

Tuesday: Alike and Different

Look at these 3 animals. How are they alike and how are they different?

Wednesday: Number Bond It!

Fill in different missing numbers in each number bond.

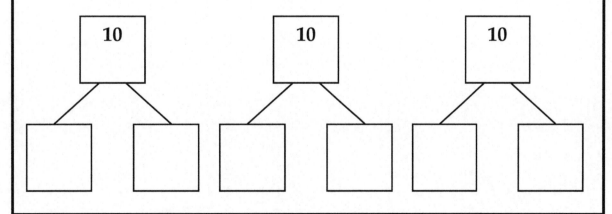

Thursday: Number Talk

What happens when you take away 0 from a number?

5 − 0
4 − 0
3 − 0
2 − 0
1 − 0

Friday: Equation Match

There were 4 dogs and 1 cat. How many are there in total?

Which equation below matches the story?

2 + 5
4 + 1
3 + 0

Week 22 Teacher Notes

Monday: 2 Arguments.

Students have to discuss which is correct.

Tuesday: Frayer Model

Students discuss the word triangle using the frayer model as a frame.

Wednesday: How Many More to

Students have to tell how many more to 7. They can count up mentally, on their fingers or use a number path or line.

Thursday: Number Talk

Students discuss solving this equation with objects, pictures and number paths or lines.

Friday: Model It!

Students model and solve the problem.

Week 22 Activities

Monday: 2 Arguments.

Listen as the teacher reads the story. Who do you think is correct? Why?

Tracie said that when you add zero to a number the number stays the same.

Kelly said the answer is 0.

Who is correct and why?

$4 + 0 = ?$

Tuesday: Frayer Model

Read the word. Discuss the different topics in the boxes based on the word.

Be sure to draw pictures of examples and nonexamples.

Triangle

Definition	Real life examples
Give a picture example	Non-examples

Wednesday: How Many More to

How many more to 7?

Start at 2
Start at 3
Start at 4
Start at 5

Thursday: Number Talk

What are some ways to think about and show:

10 – 3

1	2	3	4	5	6	7	8	9	10

Friday: Model It!

Read the story. Model it. Find the sum.

Mary had 5 big rings and 2 small rings. How many did she have altogether?

Ten frame

Picture

Answer:

Week 23 Teacher Notes

Monday: Find and Fix the Error

Students have to look at the picture and spot and discuss the errors in the numbers that were written backwards.

Tuesday: It Is/It Isn't

Students discuss the number 10. The emphasis is on the vocabulary to describe the number. Students should use expressions like greater than, less than, the same as, more than, 1 digit, 2 digit etc.

Wednesday: Number of the Day

Students fill in the boxes about the number 11.

Thursday: Number Talk

Students discuss what happens when you take away a number from itself. They should use objects, pictures and number paths or lines to figure it out.

Friday: Make Your Own Problem

Students fill in the blanks to make their own word problem. They have to then model it.

Week 23 Activities

Monday: Find and Fix the Error

Mary wrote her numbers. Which ones did she get right and which ones did she get wrong?

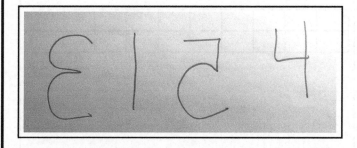

Tuesday: It Is/It Isn't

Look at the number 10 and discuss what it is and what is isn't.

10

It Is	It Isn't

Word bank: greater than, less than, same as, more than, fewer than, equals, same as, digits.

Wednesday: Number of the Day

Look at the number of the day. Fill in the squares using that number.

11

Draw 11 balls.	Draw it on the 10 frame.
Circle 11 balls.	Write the number 11.

Write up to 12. Circle 11. Put a triangle around the number that comes before 11 and underline the number that comes after 11.

Thursday: Number Talk

What are some ways to think about and show:

10 – 10

Friday: Make Your Own Problem

Fill in the blanks and make your own problem. Model and solve it.
Use numbers 2, 3, 4 or 5.
Mary had __ big rings and __ small rings. How many did she have altogether?

Ten frame

Picture

Week 24 Teacher Notes

Monday: Legs and Feet

Students have to reason about how many legs the animals have altogether.

Tuesday: More, Fewer, or the Same

Students discuss the different ways that they can describe the animals.

Wednesday: Guess My Number

Students discuss the riddle, using a number path to think and reason about the number.

Thursday: Number Talk

Students discuss doubling a number using objects and pictures.

Friday: Match the Model

Students read and discuss the story and which model matches it.

Monday: Legs and Feet

Look at the pictures and think about the problems below.

A. If we have 1 horse and 1 chicken, how many feet would there be?
B. If we have 1 horse and 2 chickens, how many feet would there be?
C. If we have 2 horses and 2 chickens, how many feet would there be?

1	2	3	4	5	6	7	8	9	10	11	12	13	14	15	16	17	18	19	20

Tuesday: More, Fewer, or the Same

Look at the pictures and discuss the animals using the words more, fewer and the same.

Wednesday: Guess My Number

Read the clues. Use them to guess the correct number.

A.	B.
I am bigger than 5. I am less than 9. I am 2 more than 6. Who am I?	I am a 2-digit number. I am less than 11. I am more than 9. Who am I?

1	2	3	4	5	6	7	8	9	10	11	12	13	14	15	16	17	18	19	20

Thursday: Number Talk

What do you notice? Use your numbers, pictures and fingers to figure out the sums.

1 + 1
2 + 2
3 + 3
4 + 4
5 + 5

Friday: Match the Model

Marvin had 3 toy trucks and 2 motorcycles. How many did he have altogether?
Which model matches the story?

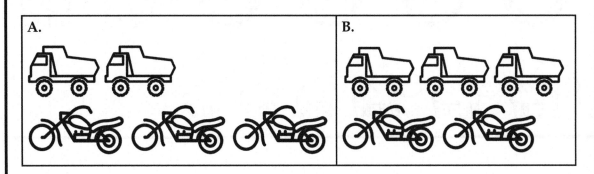

Answer:

Monday: Convince Me!

Students reason outloud about these 2 numbers using objects and pictures.

Tuesday: Frayer Model

Students discuss the word subtraction using the frayer model as a frame.

Wednesday: How Many More to

Students reason about the numbers to figure out which number is being discussed.

Thursday: Number Talk

Students explore taking 3 away from a number using counters and pictures.

Friday: Model That!

Students work on modeling the word problem.

Week 25 Activities

Monday: Convince Me!

Use numbers, words and pictures to convince me that:

5 is more than 3.

1	2	3	4	5	6	7	8	9	10

Tuesday: Frayer Model

Read the word. Discuss the different topics in the boxes based on the word.

Be sure to draw pictures of examples and non-examples.

Subtraction

What is it?	Give an example
Where do we see it in everyday life?	Non-example

Wednesday: How Many More to

How many more to 10?

Start with 9
Start with 2
Start with 3
Start with 5

Thursday: Number Talk

Use your fingers, counters and numbers to find the differences.

What are some ways to think about and show:

6 – 3
5 – 3
4 – 3
3 – 3

Friday: Model That!

Read the problem and model it. Give the answer.

Maria had 4 pink bracelets and 1 green one. How many did she have altogether?

Model on the 10 frame.

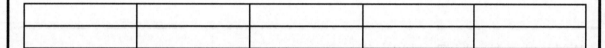

Model on the number line.

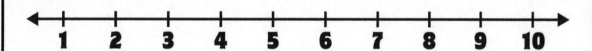

Answer:

Week 26 Teacher Notes

Monday: Reasoning Matrices

Students reason about what fruits the students like given the information they have.

Tuesday: It Is/ It Isn't

Students discuss the number 12 working with a focus on vocabulary such as more than, less than, greater than, tens, ones etc.

Wednesday: Number Bond It!

Students break apart the number 9 in different ways.

Thursday: Number Talk

Students make up their own addition problems.

Friday: What's the Story?

Students make up their own stories.

Monday: Reasoning Matrices

Listen to the information. Decide which student likes which fruit. Mark it on the table.

Carl loves grapes. Lucy does not like apples. Sue likes all fruit. Orange is Lucy's favorite color. Who likes what?

Sue			
Carl			
Lucy			

Tuesday: It Is/ It Isn't

Look at this number and talk about what it is and what it isn't. Use the word bank in your discussion.

12

It Is	It Isn't

Word bank: digit, greater than, less than, more than, tens, ones.

Wednesday: Number Bond It!

Show how to break apart 9 in 3 different ways!

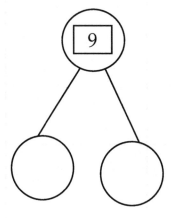 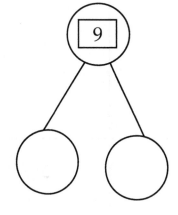 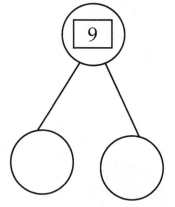

Thursday: Number Talk

Pick a number from each circle. Add them. Decide how you will solve it and write that expression under the title.

Did I do it in my head?	Did I use a model?	Did I write down the numbers and solve it on paper?

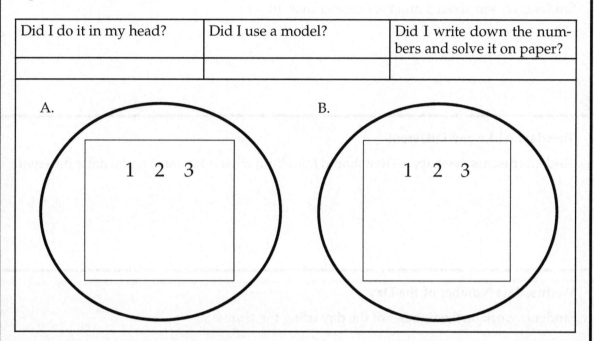

A.   B.

Friday: What's the Story?

Write a story about these insects.

Answer:

Week 27 Teacher Notes

Monday: Reasoning

Students reason about 3 numbers greater than 10.

Tuesday: Alike and Different

Students discuss the shapes. They should talk about what is the same and what is different.

Wednesday: Number of the Day

Students work on the number of the day using the template.

Thursday: Number Talk

Students make up their own problems. They use a number from each circle.

Friday: What's the Story?

Students have to tell a story about the animals. Answers vary.

Week 27 Activities

Monday: Reasoning

Name 3 numbers that are larger than 10. Explain how you know.

Tuesday: Alike and Different

Look at these 2 shapes. Talk about how they are alike and how they are different.

Word bank: sides, angles, corners (vertices), round side, straight, connecting sides, points.

Wednesday: Number of the Day

Fill in the boxes to represent the target number.

12

Write the number	Fill in the missing number. $10 + 2 =$ _____	Fill in the missing number. $12 =$ _____ $+ 2$
Ten frame	Picture Draw a picture of 12 circles. Circle 10 things and leave 2 loose.	

Fill in the number path to 12.

1	2	3	4					9			

Thursday: Number Talk

Pick a number from each circle. Subtract them. Decide how you will solve it and write that expression under the title.

Did I do it in my head?	Did I use a model?	Did I write down the numbers and solve it on paper

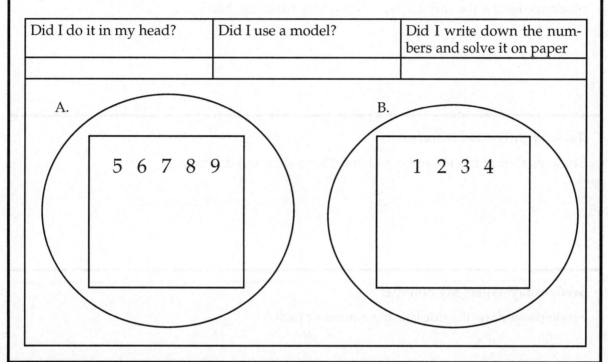

A. 5 6 7 8 9

B. 1 2 3 4

Friday: What's the Story?

Tell any kind of story about these animals.

Monday: True or False?

Students discuss the various items. Then they make up their own.

Tuesday: Alike and Different

Students should talk about how 12 and 15 are alike and different.

Wednesday: Guess My Number

Students work on the riddle using a number path.

Thursday: Number Strings

Students discuss this problem using objects, pictures and the number path.

Friday: Problem Solving

Students discuss this problem and draw pictures to illustrate it.

Week 28 Activities

Monday: True or False?

Look at each problem. Decide if it is true or false. Discuss why.

True or False	True or False	Make Your Own and Share It out
This is a circle	This is not a square	

Tuesday: Alike and Different

Talk about how these numbers are alike and different.

12 and 15

Alike	Different

Word bank: greater than, less than, more than, fewer than, same as, equal to, digits.

Wednesday: Guess My Number

Listen to the clues. Use them to figure out what the correct number is.

I am a 2-digit number.
I am more than 12.
I am less than 15.
My digits add up to 5.
Who am I?

1	2	3	4	5	6	7	8	9	10	11	12	13	14	15	16	17	18	19	20

Thursday: Number Strings

What are some ways to think about:
9 – 5?

Friday: Problem Solving

At the aquarium, we saw turtles and fish. We saw 4 animals. Draw what we could have seen.

Draw it with green and yellow crayons.

		Draw the pictures. Use a green and an orange crayon to draw circles for your pictures.
4	0	
3	2	
2	1	
1	0	
0	1	

Week 29 Teacher Notes

Monday: 2 Arguments

In this routine, students have to think about the thinking of others. They should be encouraged to choose who they think is correct and then have to prove it with numbers, words and pictures.

Tuesday: Alike and Different

In this routine, students are comparing 3 different shapes. The emphasis should be on the attributes of polygons.

Wednesday: Number Scramble

In this routine, students have to unscramble the numbers and put them in the correct sequence on the number path.

Thursday: Number Talk

In this routine, students are making their own addition problems and then discussing how they solved them.

Friday: What's the Question?

In this routine, students are going to tell word problems based on the answer. The teacher should give the students an opportunity to think on their own, then with a partner and finally with the whole class.

Week 29 Activities

Monday: 2 Arguments

Listen to the story. Discuss and then decide who you think is correct. Explain why.

Sue said that 8 take away 2 is 7. Mia said that it was 6.

Who is correct?

Prove it.

Tuesday: Alike and Different

Compare these shapes.
How are they alike?
How are they different?

 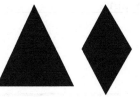

Wednesday: Number Scramble

Put these numbers in order on the number path.

7   2   5   1   4   8   9   10   3   6

Thursday: Number Talk

Pick a number from each circle. Make a subtraction problem. Write the problem under the way you solved it.

Did I do it in my head?	Did I use a model?	Did I write down the numbers and solve it on paper?

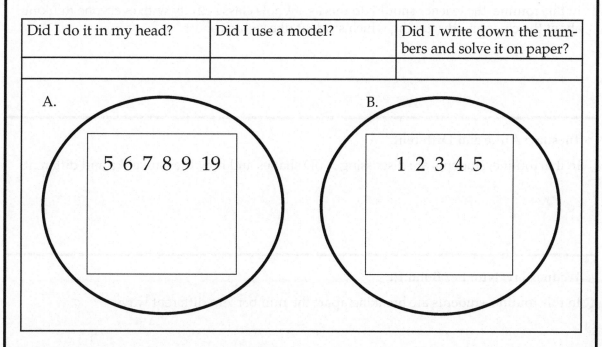

A.

5 6 7 8 9 19

B.

1 2 3 4 5

Friday: What's the Question?

The answer is 1 cat. What is the question?

Week 30 Teacher Notes

Monday: Reasoning Matrices

In this routine, the teacher should do this as a whole class activity with everyone thinking about the clues and discussing which student likes which sport.

Tuesday: Alike and Different

In this routine, students are discussing 3, 3D shapes and how they are alike and different.

Wednesday: Number Bond It!

In this routine, students are breaking apart the number 7 in different ways.

Thursday: Number Strings

In this number string, students are discussing what it means to take a number away from itself.

Friday: Model That!

In this routine, students are modeling the problem in a variety of ways. They should also write the answer.

Monday: Reasoning Matrices

Listen to the story. Decide which toy which child likes to play with.

Carl loves to play with vehicles. Lucy loves ball games. Sue likes all toys. Who likes what?

Sue			
Carl			
Lucy			

Tuesday: Alike and Different

Discuss the solids and decide how they are alike and how they are different.

Wednesday: Number Bond It!

Show how to break apart 7 in 3 different ways!

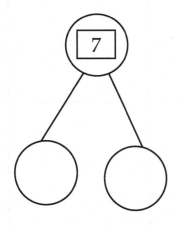 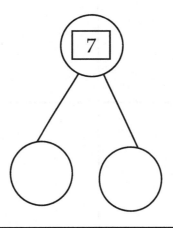 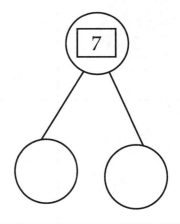

Thursday: Number Strings

What are some ways to think about these problems?

5 – 5   7 – 7   10 – 10

Friday: Model That!

In the aquarium there were 5 fish. There were 4 turtles. How many animals are there in total?

Model it with a picture.

Model it on the 10 frame.

Circle the correct equation.

$5 + 0 = 5$ $5 + 4 = 9$ $6 + 3 = 9$

Week 31 Teacher Notes

Monday: Composing Numbers

In this routine, students are composing numbers to 5.

Tuesday: Frayer Model

In this routine, students are discussing a rectangle. They should talk about the definition, draw a picture, discuss where we see them in real life and give a non example.

Wednesday: How Many More to

In this routine, students are discussing how to get from a given number to 10.

Thursday: Number Talk

In this routine, students are working on making up their own subtraction problems and discussing their strategies for solving them.

Friday: What's the Question?

In this problem, students are making up word problems where the answer is 3 dogs. Discuss the answer with the students and then give them "think time" on their own and then with a partner. Then, have the class come back together and share their ideas with the whole class and discuss the different stories. The teacher should try to get both addition and subtraction stories.

Week 31 Activities

Monday: Composing Numbers

Color in the rectangles to show 4 different ways to make 5.

Tuesday: Frayer Model

Read the word. Discuss the different topics in the boxes based on the word.

Be sure to draw pictures of examples and nonexamples.

Rectangle

What is it?	What does it look like?
Where do we see them in real life?	What is it not?

Wednesday: How Many More to

10

Start at 1 …

Start at 2 …

Start at 8 …

Start at 9 …

Thursday: Number Talk

Pick a number from each circle. Make a subtraction problem. Write the problem under the way you solved it.

Did I do it in my head?	Did I use a model?	Did I write down the numbers and solve it on paper

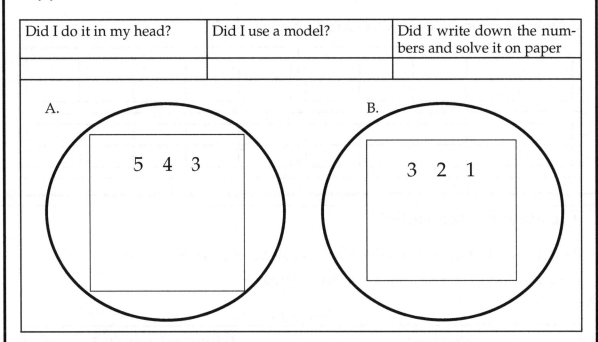

A.   5   4   3

B.   3   2   1

Friday: What's the Question?

The answer is 3 dogs. What was the question?

Monday: Composing Numbers

In this routine, students are composing the number 6 in a variety of ways.

Tuesday: Frayer Model

In this routine, students are discussing what the word graph means. They will discuss what it is, give examples, talk about how we use them in everyday life and then give non examples.

Wednesday: Greater Than, Less Than, in Between

In this routine, students will talk about the relationship between numbers. They will explore concepts of close, far and in between.

Thursday: Number Talk

In this routine, students get to make their own subtraction problems. After they solve them, they will discuss their strategies.

Friday: What's the Question?

In this routine, students have to come up with good questions after listening to the story.

As a class, you read the problem 3 times. The first time you discuss the story. The second time you discuss the numbers. The third time the students make up questions and answer them.

Week 32 Activities

Monday: Composing Numbers

Color in the rectangles to show 4 different ways to make 6.

Tuesday: Frayer Model

Fill in the boxes based on the word.

Graph

Definition	Examples
Give a picture example	**Non-examples**

Wednesday: Greater Than, Less Than, in Between

Use the numbers to fill in the boxes.

1   10   7

Name a number more than 1	Name a number less than 10	Name a number more than 7
Name a number less than 7	Name a number in between 1 and 10	Name a number in between 7 and 10

Thursday: Number Talk

Pick a number from each circle. Make a subtraction problem. Write the problem under the way you solved it.

Did I do it in my head?	Did I use a model?	Did I write down the numbers and solve it on paper

A.

5   4   3

B.

3   2   1   0

Friday: What's the Question?

Read the story 3 times with your class.

Think of at least 2 questions you could ask about this story. Discuss with your classmates.

Mary has 1 blue ring and 3 yellow rings.

1)

2)

Week 33 Teacher Notes

Monday: Composing Numbers

In this routine, students are composing 7 in different ways.

Tuesday: Frayer Model

In this routine, students are discussing what the word compare means. They will talk about the definition, draw an example, talk about how we use it in real life and give a non example.

Wednesday: Number of the Day

In this routine, students will be exploring the number 9 and different ways to represent it.

Thursday: Number Talk

In this routine, students will be exploring a number string of subtracting 3 from a number. The emphasis should be on the count back strategy.

Friday: Both Addends Unknown

In this routine, students are looking at the both addends unknown problem type. They should draw pictures to match the table.

Monday: Composing Numbers

How many ways?

Color in the rectangles to show 4 different ways to make 7.

Tuesday: Frayer Model

Read the word. Discuss the different topics in the boxes based on the word.
Be sure to draw pictures of examples and nonexamples.

Compare

Definition	Examples
Give a picture example	Non-examples

Wednesday: Number of the Day

Fill in the boxes to represent the target number.

9

Write the number.	Make a picture of 9 things.
Circle the 9 on the number ladder. 1 2 3 4 5 6 7 8 9	Write an addition sentence that makes 9. Write a subtraction sentence that has a difference of 9. ___ + ___ = 9 ___ − ___ = 9

Write numbers 1 through 10 on the number line. Circle the number that comes before 9 and underline the number that comes after it.

Thursday: Number Talk

How can we think about these problems: 10 – 3
9 – 3
8 – 3
7 – 3

1	2	3	4	5	6	7	8	9	10

Friday: Both Addends Unknown

At the zoo, there were zebras and monkeys. There were 5 animals altogether. There was at least one of each.

🦓	🐵	Draw the pictures to show the combinations. You can use a black crayon and a brown crayon to draw circles for the pictures.
1	4	
2	3	
3	2	
4	1	

Monday: Composing Numbers

In this routine, students are composing the number 8 in different ways.

Tuesday: Draw and Discuss

Students draw and discuss 2D shapes.

Wednesday: Number Scramble

In this routine, students have to look at the different number sequences and decide which one is correct.

Thursday: Number Talk

In this number talk students get to choose their own numbers and make subtraction problems. They then have to discuss how they solved them.

Friday: What's the Story?

Students use the picture prompts to tell a part-part whole story.

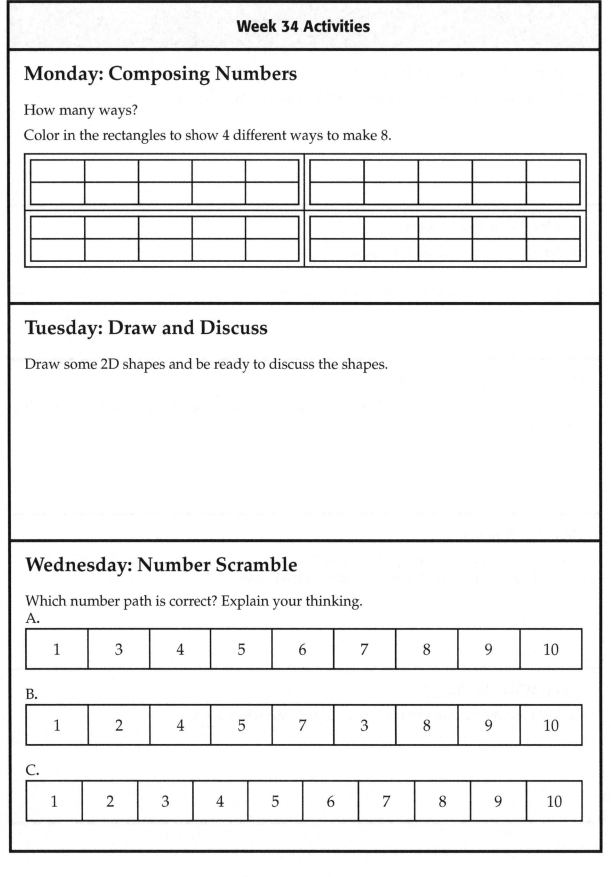

Week 34 Activities

Monday: Composing Numbers

How many ways?

Color in the rectangles to show 4 different ways to make 8.

Tuesday: Draw and Discuss

Draw some 2D shapes and be ready to discuss the shapes.

Wednesday: Number Scramble

Which number path is correct? Explain your thinking.

A.

| 1 | 3 | 4 | 5 | 6 | 7 | 8 | 9 | 10 |

B.

| 1 | 2 | 4 | 5 | 7 | 3 | 8 | 9 | 10 |

C.

| 1 | 2 | 3 | 4 | 5 | 6 | 7 | 8 | 9 | 10 |

Thursday: Number Talk

Pick a number from each circle. Subtract them. Decide how you will solve it and write that expression under the title.

Did I do it in my head?	Did I use a model?	Did I write down the numbers and solve it on paper

A.

10 9 8 7 6

B.

5 4 3 2 1

Friday: What's the Story?

Tell a story about this picture. It can be a join story or a take away story. Model your thinking and write the answer.

Monday: Composing Numbers

In this routine, students are composing numbers to 9.

Tuesday: Frayer Model

In this routine, students are discussing a square. They will define it, draw an example, discuss where they see them in real life and give non-examples.

Wednesday: Number of the Day

In this routine, students will be discussing the number 14 and how to represent it in a variety of ways.

Thursday: Number Strings

In this number string, students will be discussing how many more to 10.

Friday: Make Your Own Problem

In this routine, students get to pick their own numbers to make a problem and then solve it.

Week 35 Activities

Monday: Composing Numbers

Color in the rectangles to show 4 different ways to make 9.

Tuesday: Frayer Model

Fill in the boxes based on the word.

Square

Definition	Examples
Give a picture example	**Non-examples**

Wednesday: Number of the Day

Look at the number of the day. Fill in the squares using that number.

14

Write the number.	Write the missing number. $14 = 10 + \underline{}$	Write the missing number. $4 + \underline{} = 14$
Break apart 14 in the number bond.	Represent 14 on the double ten frame.	Draw 14 circles.

Thursday: Number Strings

Look at the problems below. Discuss how many more to 10. Use different models, including your fingers, number lines, and pictures.

$1 + \underline{} = 10$
$2 + \underline{} = 10$
$3 + \underline{} = 10$
$4 + \underline{} = 10$
$5 + \underline{} = 10$

1	2	3	4	5	6	7	8	9	10

Friday: Make Your Own Problem

Pick numbers between 0 and 5 to fill in the spaces.

The store had _____ rings. It got _____ more. How many does it have now?

Model it!

Monday: Composing Numbers

In this routine, students are composing 10 in different ways.

Tuesday: Alike and Different

In this routine, students are talking about the similarities and differences between a square and a triangle. The emphasis should be on discussing the attributes of polygons – closed figures, vertices, straight lines etc.

Wednesday: What Doesn't Belong?

In this routine, students are discussing addition facts.

Thursday: Number Talk

In this routine, students are discussing strategies for subtracting a number from 10.

Friday: What's the Problem?

In this routine, students look at the empty donut box provided and tell a subtraction story.

Monday: Composing Numbers

Color in the rectangles to show 4 different ways to make 10.

Tuesday: Alike and Different

Discuss how these 2 shapes are alike and how they are different.

Wednesday: What Doesn't Belong?

Look at the set of numbers. Discuss and decide which one doesn't belong and why.

5 + 5	7 + 3
1 + 9	6 + 2

Thursday: Number Talk

What are some ways to solve:

10 – 8
10 – 7
10 – 6
10 – 5

1	2	3	4	5	6	7	8	9	10

Friday: What's the Problem?

If the answer is 0, what could the problem be?

Monday: What Doesn't Belong?

In this routine, students first discuss numbers. Then they discuss subtraction problems.

Tuesday: It Is/It Isn't

In this routine, students discuss what 15 is and isn't. They should be using words like 1 digit versus 2 digit number. They should be discussing how it has a ten and five ones. They should talk about how it is a teen number. They can talk about what it is greater and less than as well.

Wednesday: Greater Than, Less Than, in Between

In this routine, students are talking about and comparing numbers. They discuss what they are close to, what they are far from and what comes in between them.

Thursday: Number Strings

In this number talk, students are looking at lower half facts. They can be making connections between lower doubles and half facts.

Friday: What's the Story?

In this routine, the students are given a 10 frame and asked to tell a story about the number that is modeled on it.

Monday: What Doesn't Belong?

Look at the set of numbers. Discuss and decide which one doesn't belong and why.

A.

11	14
18	9

B.

6 − 3	5 − 2
4 − 1	5 − 3

Tuesday: It Is/It Isn't

Discuss the number 15. Use the word bank.

15

It Is	It Isn't

Word bank: greater than, less than, in between, digits, same as, equals.

Wednesday: Greater Than, Less Than, in Between

Look at the boxes and fill in the correct answers about the numbers.

2 12 20

Name a number less than 2	Name a number greater than 12	Name a number less than 20
Name a number greater than 2	Name a number in between 2 and 12	Name a number in between 12 and 20

Thursday: Number Strings

Think about these expressions. Use your fingers, a ten frame and pictures to think about the difference.

$4 - 2$
$6 - 3$
$8 - 4$
$10 - 5$

Friday: What's the Story?

Look at the picture. Tell a story about this model. It can be a join story or a take away story.

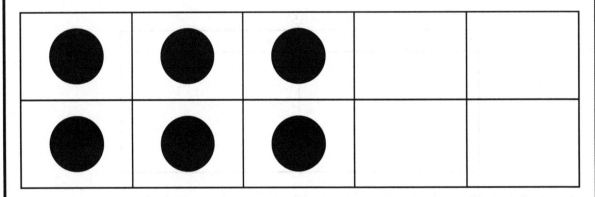

Monday: What Doesn't Belong?

In this activity students are working on addition and subtraction. The students can think about the different problems using their fingers, counters, 10 frames and number lines.

Tuesday: Frayer Model

In this activity students are discussing teen numbers. They will talk about what they are, give examples, discuss where we see them in real life and discuss non-examples as well.

Wednesday: Number of the Day

In this activity students will represent the number 19 in different ways.

Thursday: Number Talk

In this number talk, students will make up their own problems. They will choose numbers from each circle and decide whether they want to add or subtract. They will then solve their problem and discuss how they did it.

Friday: Word Problem Sort

Which one is the take away problem?

Monday: What Doesn't Belong?

Look at the set of numbers. Discuss and decide which one doesn't belong and why.

A.

1 + 4	2 + 3
6 − 1	10 − 3

B.

9 − 3	6 − 0
5 + 1	10 − 6

Tuesday: Frayer Model

Fill in the boxes based on the word.

Teen numbers

What are they?	Examples
Where do we see them in real life?	Non-examples

Wednesday: Number of the Day

Fill in the boxes to represent the target number.

19

Write the number	Write the missing number. 19 = 10 + ___	Write the missing number. 9 + ___ = 19
Break apart 19 into the number bond.	Represent 19 in the double ten frame.	Draw 19 circles. Circle a group of 10 and leave 9 loose.

Thursday: Number Talk

Pick a number from each circle. Make a problem. Decide how you will solve it and write that expression under the title.

Did I do it in my head?	Did I use a model?	Did I write down the numbers and solve it on paper

A.

1 2 3 4 5

B.

5 4 3 2 1

Friday: Word Problem Sort

Which one is the take away problem?

Sue has 7 marbles. She gave 3 away. How many does she have now?	Sue has 7 marbles. She got 3 more from her sister. How many does she have now?

Week 39 Teacher Notes

Monday: Reasoning Matrix

The teacher talks with the students about each square. Together the class decides who likes to do what.

Tuesday: Number Talk

Students have to pick 2 numbers and describe how they solved the problem.

Wednesday: Guess My Number

These are thinking riddles to get students to reason about numbers.

Thursday: Number Talk

Students get to make their own problems. They can make addition or subtraction problems.

Friday: What's the Story?

Students have to tell, model and solve a story.

Monday: Reasoning Matrix

Read the clues and figure out what is the favorite sport of each student.

Carl loves the ice. Lucy does not love to walk. Sue likes to do a lot of things. Who likes what?

	🚲	⛸	🚶
Sue			
Carl			
Lucy			

Tuesday: Number Talk

Fill in the box based on the word.

3D shape

Definition	Examples
Give a picture example	Non-examples

Wednesday: Guess My Number

Read the clues. Use them to guess the correct number.

A.	B.
I am bigger than 17. I am less than 20. My digits add to 10. Who am I?	I am a 1-digit number. I am less than 10. I am more than 7. I am the sum of 4 + 4. Who am I?

Thursday: Number Talk

Pick a number from each circle. Make a problem. Decide how you will solve it and write that expression under the title.

Did I do it in my head?	Did I use a model?	Did I write down the numbers and solve it on paper

A.

0 1 2 3 4 5

B.

0 1 2 3 4 5

Friday: What's the Story?

Tell an addition story about turtles and fish. Use the numbers 0, 1, 2, 3, 4, or 5.

Draw it!

Monday: 3 Truths and a Fib

In this activity students have to reason about a series of statements, 3 of which are true and 1 of which is false. It is important to reason about each of the statements with the students and have them think about them while looking at the number path and the 10 frame model.

Tuesday: Brainstorm

In this activity, students discuss measurement. They can write and draw pictures in the clouds that illustrate measurement.

Wednesday: Number of the Day

In this activity students work on representing the number 20 in a variety of ways.

Thursday: Number Talk

In this activity students get to choose their own numbers and make their own problems. The teacher asks students how they solved it. Answers will vary. Some students will do it in their head, others will do it on a model and some will write it down on paper.

Friday: What's the Question?

In this problem, the teacher reads it 3 times. The first time the class discusses the situation. The second time, they talk about what the numbers mean. The third time they talk about what questions they could ask. Then, they discuss the answers.

How many cookies are there altogether?
Are there more sugar cookies or lemon ones?
Which has the most?
Which has the least?
How many more lemon cookies would we need to have the same amount of sugar cookies.

Monday: 3 Truths and a Fib

Which one is false? Why? Explain to your neighbor and then the group.

3 is bigger than 7	17 is bigger than 10
4 is 1 more than 3	10 is less than 12

Tuesday: Brainstorm

In each thought cloud write or draw something that has to do with measurement.

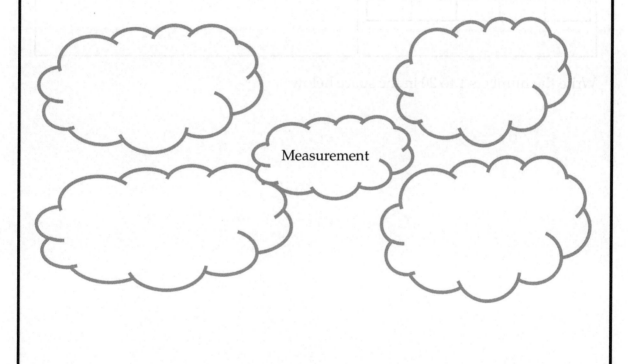

Measurement

Wednesday: Number of the Day

Fill in the boxes to represent the target number.

20

Write the number.	Solve $10 + 10 = \_\_\_\_$
Represent 20 on the ten frame.	Draw a picture of 20 things. Circle groups of 10.

Write the numbers 1 to 20 in the space below.

Thursday: Number Talk

Pick a number from each circle. Make a problem. Decide how you will solve it and write that expression under the title.

Did I do it in my head?	Did I use a model?	Did I write down the numbers and solve it on paper.

A.

1 2 3 4 5 0

B.

1 2 3 4 5 0

Friday: What's the Question?

Read the story 3 times with your class. Ask some questions about it.

The bakery had 2 lemon cookies and 5 sugar cookies.	What are some questions that you can ask?

Answer Key

Week 1
Monday: What Doesn't Belong? A. A. B. giraffe.
Tuesday: Alike and Different They are alike because they have straight lines, they are closed figures, and they have corners (vertices). They are different because the triangle has 3 sides and the square has 4 sides. The triangle has 3 corners and the square has 4.
Wednesday: Number of the Day Draw a picture; draw in the 10 frame and mark on the number path.
Thursday: Number Talk Students should show 3 fingers in different ways.
Friday: What's the Story? There were 3 giraffes and 1 more came. Now there are 4 giraffes.

Week 2

Monday: What Doesn't Belong?

Answers vary. In A we could say the frog is the only one that is a reptile. The cow is the only one that can have horns. The kangaroo is the only one that has a pouch. For B, the giraffe is the only one that has spots. The zebra is the only one that has stripes. The kangaroo is the only one that has a pouch.

Tuesday: Alike and Different

Students discuss how the sphere is round and the cone is curved and how they both roll.

Wednesday: Number Scramble

C.

Thursday: Number Talk

Students show 4 on their fingers in different ways.

Friday: Problem Solving

There were 4 giraffes. 1 more came. Now there are 5 giraffes.

Week 3

Monday: Counting Jar

Answers vary.

Tuesday: More, Less, or the Same

There are more butterflies. There are fewer ladybugs than butterflies.

Wednesday: True or False

This is a circle. Circles are round. They don't have straight sides.

Thursday: Number Talk

Students show 5 on their fingers in different ways.

Friday: Problem Solving

There were 2 cows. 2 more came. Now there are 4 cows.

Week 4

Monday: Counting Arrangements

Students should be able to count the amounts in different arrangements.

A. 4.

B. 4.

C. 4.

D. 8.

E. 6.

F. 6.

Tuesday: Positional Words

Students act out positional vocabulary.

Wednesday: Convince Me!

Students discuss and prove with objects and pictures that 3 is more than 1.

Thursday: Number Talk

Students show 6 on their fingers in different ways.

Friday: Problem Solving

6 ladybugs.

Week 5

Monday: What Doesn't Belong?

Cone; B.

Tuesday: More, Less, or the Same

More butterflies (4); fewer ladybugs (3) and bees (3). Same bees and ladybugs.

Wednesday: Number of the Day

Students write the number, draw a picture and show it on a 10 frame.

Thursday: Number Talk

Students show different representations of 7 on their fingers, answers vary.

Friday: Problem Solving

6 ladybugs.

Week 6

Monday: Counting Jars

Estimate the items in the jar; answers vary.

Tuesday: Positional Words

Students act out the positional vocabulary.

Wednesday: Number of the Day

Write the number 5; show 5 in the 10 frame; draw a picture of 5 things.

Thursday: Number Talk

Students should discuss when you add 1 to a number it increases the number to the next number – 3, 4, 5, and 6.

Friday: Problem Solving

Answers vary. For example, there were 4 dogs and 1 more came.

Week 7

Monday: Counting Jar

Estimate the items in the jar; answers vary.

Tuesday: Positional Words

Answers vary for the shape beside the circle.

Wednesday: Number of the Day

Write the number 6; show 6 in the 10 frame; draw a picture of 6 things.

Thursday: Number Talk

Students should discuss that when you add 0 to a number the number stays the same.

Friday: Problem Solving

Stories vary. Students can tell join or take away stories. For example: There were 2 elephants and 2 more came. How many elephants are there now? There were 4 elephants and 2 left. How many are there now? (They can model this by putting an x through 2 of them.)

Week 8

Monday: Counting Arrangements

A. 5.

B. 7.

C. 9.

D. 5.

Tuesday: Positional Words

Students act out the words.

Wednesday: Convince Me!

They could draw pictures, a number line or a ten frame, or something else.

Thursday: Number Talk

Students discuss ways to make 8.

Friday: Problem Solving

4 monkeys.

Week 9

Monday: What Doesn't Belong

A. Answers vary. The bird flies. The frog lives on land and in water. The kangaroo has a pouch.

B. The monkey lives in trees. The zebra has stripes. The butterfly is an insect. The giraffe has a long neck.

Tuesday: Alike and Different

They are alike because they are both animals with ears, mouths and eyes. They are different because the zebra has 4 legs and the monkey has two legs. The zebra has stripes and the monkey doesn't. The monkey lives in trees and the zebra lives on the ground.

Wednesday: Number of the Day

Write the number 7; place 7 in the 10 frame; draw a picture of 7 things.

Thursday: Number Talk

Students discuss ways to make 5.

Friday: Problem Solving

1 monkey.

Week 10

Monday: Counting Fingers

A. 8.

B. 4.

C. 2.

D. 6.

Tuesday: Counting Words

Students count to 20 and discuss the counting words.

A. 9.

B. 14.

C. 19.

D. Answers vary.

Wednesday: Number of the Day

Write the number 8; place it in the 10 frame; draw 8 things.

Thursday: Number Talk

1 and 6; 2 and 5; 4 and 3; 6 and 1; 5 and 2; and 3 and 4.

Friday: Problem Solving

2 zebras.

Week 11

Monday: Counting Jar

Estimate the items in the jar.

Tuesday: More, Less or the Same

There are the same amount of apples and bananas.

Wednesday: True or False?

Students have to prove that 2 is not more than 3 with numbers, words and pictures.

Thursday: Number Talk

2 and 6; 1 and 7; 3 and 5; 6 and 2; 7 and 1; 5 and 3; 4 and 4.

Friday: Problem Solving

Students have to tell a story that matches the model. For example: there were 5 elephants and 3 left. Now there are 2 elephants.

Week 12

Monday: Counting Arrangements

Students count the cats in different arrangements. There are 4 in all the arrangements.

Tuesday: Positional Words

Answers visual.

Wednesday: Convince Me!

Students have to talk about 8 and 10.

Thursday: Number Talk

1 and 8; 2 and 7; 3 and 6; 4 and 5; 8 and 1; 7 and 2; 6 and 3; 5 and 4; 6 and 3.

Friday: Problem Solving

Students need to model the answer in different ways.

Week 13

Monday: What Doesn't Belong?

Triangle; cow.

Tuesday: Alike and Different

They are different because the cow is a mammal and the butterfly is an insect; one flies and one walks. They are alike because they are living creatures.

Wednesday: Number of the Day

Write the number 10; show 10 in the number frame; draw 10 things.

Thursday: Number Talk

1 and 9; 2 and 8; 3 and 7; 4 and 6; 5 and 5; 9 and 1; 8 and 2; 7 and 3; 6 and 4.

Friday: Problem Solving

The answer is 3. Students need to model the answer in different ways.

Week 14

Monday: Finger Counting

A. 6.

B. 3.

C. 6.

D. 5.

Tuesday: Counting Words

Students work on number words and counting.

After 9 is 10.

After 10 is 11.

After 19 is 20.

After 29 is 30.

Wednesday: Number Bond It!

Students break apart 4 in different ways. For example 3 and 1; 2 and 2; 1 and 3.

Thursday: Number Strings

Students discuss counting on from the big number.

Friday: Problem Solving

0 whales left. Students need to model the answer in different ways.

Week 15

Monday: Counting Jar

Answers vary.

Tuesday: Frayer Model

Students discuss what numbers are using the frame of the frayer model.

Wednesday: True or False?

Students discuss that this is a rectangle because it has 4 sides, 4 angles and 4 vertices. They should talk about how it is closed and the sides are straight.

Thursday: Number Talk

Students discuss counting back.

Friday: Problem Solving

1 giraffe left. Students need to model the answer in different ways.

Week 16

Monday: Counting Arrangements

There are 10 items no matter how they are arranged.

Tuesday: Vocabulary

Name the shapes you know (circle, triangle, square); answers vary.

Wednesday: Convince Me!

Students discuss the numbers using objects and pictures.

Thursday: Number Talk

It becomes zero.

Friday: Problem Solving

Students need to model the answer in different ways. The answer is 4.

Week 17

Monday: What Doesn't Belong?

$0 + 2$

Tuesday: Alike and Different

They are shapes with straight sides and points. They have different amounts of sides and points.

Wednesday: Number of the Day

Students write, draw and illustrate 10 in a 10 frame.

Thursday: Number Talk

The number remains the same.

Friday: Problem Solving

Students need to model the answer in different ways. The answer is 0.

Week 18

Monday: Finger Counting

A. 9.

B. 7.

C. 10.

D. 8.

Tuesday: Before and After

9, 9, 19, 16 ... students are working on the vocabulary of before and after.

Wednesday: Number Bond It!

Students break apart 6 in different ways. For example: 5 and 1; 2 and 4; 3 and 3.

Thursday: Number Talk

Students continue to discuss counting on 2 more from the largest number.

Friday: Problem Solving

2 cats. Students need to model the answer in different ways.

Week 19

Monday: Counting Jar

Answers vary.

Tuesday: Frayer Model

Students discuss the word sum using the frayer model.

Wednesday: True or False?

Students discuss whether or not the equation is true or false. They should use numbers, words and pictures to explain their thinking. The answer is true.

Thursday: Number Talk

It decreases by 2; show it on the number line.

Friday: Problem Solving

7 altogether. Students need to model the answer in different ways.

Week 20

Monday: Counting Arrangements

Students should discuss that no matter what the arrangement, the amount is 8.

Tuesday: Vocabulary

Students discuss number words. Answers vary. For example: two, ten and fifty.

Wednesday: Convince Me!

Students discuss and prove the equation with objects and pictures.

Thursday: Number Talk

Students discuss subtracting from 10. In kindergarten they can use their fingers as models. Some students might begin to relate subtracting from ten to adding ten pairs. For example if $5 + 5$ is 10, then $10 - 5$ is 5.

Friday: Problem Solving

7 altogether. Students need to model the answer in different ways.

Week 21

Monday: What Doesn't Belong?

1 + 0. Some students could say 1 + 1 is the only doubles fact and also it is the only expression that does not have a zero in it.

Tuesday: Alike and Different

Answers vary. They are all mammals. The zebra is the only one that has stripes. The giraffe is the only one that has spots. The lion has a mane.

Wednesday: Number Bond It!

Students break apart 10 in different ways. For example: 9 and 1; 8 and 2; 7 and 3.

Thursday: Number Talk

Students discuss taking 0 from a number and how the number always stays the same.

Friday: Equation Match

5 altogether. 4 + 1.

Week 22

Monday: 2 Arguments

Tracie.

Tuesday: Frayer Model

Students discuss a triangle using the frayer model.

Wednesday: How Many More to

2 + 5; 3 + 4; 4 + 3; 5 + 2.

Thursday: Number Talk

Visual – show fingers, draw a picture, show in 10 frame.

Friday: Model It!

7, show in 10 frame, have students draw pictures.

Week 23

Monday: Find and Fix the Error

3 and 5 are written backwards.

Tuesday: It Is/It Isn't

Answers vary. 10 is a 2 digit number; it is more than 5; it is less than 20; it is not a 1 digit number; it is not more than 11. It is not less than 2.

Wednesday: Number of the Day

Students draw 11 balls and draw 11 on the double 10 frame. They fill in all the representations in the activity.

Thursday: Number Talk

Answers vary.

Friday: Make Your Own Problem

Answers vary.

Week 24

Monday: Legs and Feet

A. 6.

B. 8.

C. 10.

Tuesday: More, Less or the Same

Students discuss the animals. There are more zebras than monkeys. There are more monkeys than giraffes. There are fewer giraffes than monkeys. Answers vary.

Wednesday: Guess My Number

A. 8.

B. 10.

Thursday: Number Talk

Students should discuss doubles.

Friday: Match the Model

B.

They had 5 altogether.

Week 25
Monday: Convince Me! Visual with discussion – use fingers, drawings, and objects to explain 5 is more than 3.
Tuesday: Frayer Model Students discuss subtraction using the frayer model as a frame. Answers vary: What is it? It is when you take away a number from another number. Example: 4 – 2; Non-example: 2 + 2; everyday life: We spend money.
Wednesday: How Many More to 1, 8, 7, 5.
Thursday: Number Talk Visual – use fingers, drawings, objects.
Friday: Model That 5; show on 10 frame, model on number line.

Week 26

Monday: Reasoning Matrices

Check grapes for Carl; Check oranges for Lucy; Check apples for Sue.

Tuesday: It Is/It Isn't

12 is greater that 10; it isn't more than 13; answers vary.

Wednesday: Number Bond It!

Answers vary. For example: 8 and 1; 7 and 2; 5 and 4.

Thursday: Number Talk

Answers vary. For example 3 + 3 = 6. 2 + 2 = 4.

Friday: What's the Story?

Answers vary. For example: There were 4 ladybugs and 3 butterflies. How many insects were there altogether? There were 7 insects, 5 left. How many are there now?

Week 27

Monday: Reasoning Matrices

Answers vary, example 12, 13, 14 or 11, 12, 15 – verbal interaction.

Tuesday: Alike and Different

They both have straight sides. They both have points. They have different amounts of straight sides.

Wednesday: Number of the Day

Students fill in the number of the day template using the number.

Thursday: Number Talk

For example: $5 - 4 = 1$; $4 - 4 = 0$; $3 - 1 = 2$.

Friday: What's the Story?

Answers vary. For example: There were 4 zebras and 4 monkeys. How many animals are there altogether? There were 8 animals and 4 left. How many are there now?

Week 28

Monday: True or False?

False, true, answers vary.

Tuesday: Alike and Different

12 and 15 are numbers. They are both greater than 10. They are both less than 20. 12 is in between 11 and 13. 15 is in between 14 and 16.

Wednesday: Guess My Number

14

Thursday: Number Strings

Students should solve with objects and pictures.

Friday: Problem Solving

Students draw the pictures.

Week 29

Monday: 2 Arguments

Mia. Students discuss this with objects and pictures. Answers vary.

Tuesday: Alike and Different

Students discuss how they all have straight sides and corners but different amounts of sides and corners. Answers vary.

Wednesday: Number Scramble

Students put the numbers on the number path in the correct order.

Thursday: Number Talk

Answers vary. For example: $6 - 1 = 5$; $8 - 8 = 0$; $10 - 1 = 9$.

Friday: What's the Question?

Answers may vary. For example: There were 4 cats in the house. Three cats left. How many are still in the house? 1 cat.

Week 30

Monday: Reasoning Matrices

Carl likes the truck; Lucy likes soccer and marbles; Sue likes marbles.

Tuesday: Alike and Different

Students discuss the similarities and differences of the shapes. They all roll. The cylinder and the cone have flat sides. Answers vary.

Wednesday: Number Bond It!

Students break apart 7 in different ways. Answers vary. For example: 6 and 1; 5 and 2; 4 and 3.

Thursday: Number Strings

Verbal discussion; when you take away a number from itself you get zero.

Friday: Model That

Models vary. 5 + 4 = 9.

Week 31

Monday: Composing Numbers

Answers will vary. Use crayons to show ways to make 5. For example 4 and 1; 3 and 2; 2 and 3.

Tuesday: Frayer Model

Students discuss the word rectangle using the frayer model as a frame. Answers vary. For example: What is it: It is a shape with 4 sides. It has 4 corners. The sides are straight. What does it look like? students draw a picture of a rectangle. Real life: rug. What it is not: circle.

Wednesday: How Many More to

$1 + 9; 2 + 8; 8 + 2; 9 + 1$.

Thursday: Number Talk

Answers will vary. For example: $5 - 3 = 2; 3 - 2 = 1$.

Friday: What's the Question?

Answers will vary. Example: There were 6 dogs. 3 went to the dog park. How many stayed at home?

Week 32

Monday: Composing Numbers

Answers will vary. Color 4 different ways to make 6. For example: 5 and 1; 4 and 2; 3 and 3.

Tuesday: Frayer Model

Students discuss the word graph using the frayer model as a frame.

Answers vary. For example:

Definition: A way to show data.

Example: Weather Graph.

Non-example: Circle.

Sketch: (students sketch it).

Wednesday: Greater Than, Less Than, in Between

Answers will vary; for example, 2 is more than 1; 9 is less than 10 and 5 is in between 1 and 10.

Thursday: Number Talk

Answers will vary. For example: 5-5; 4–1; 3–2.

Friday: What's the Question?

Verbal discussion, example: How many rings does she have altogether? How many fewer blue rings did she have than yellow ones?

Week 33

Monday: Composing Numbers

Answers will vary, color 4 different ways to make 7. For example: 6 and 1; 5 and 2; 3 and 4.

Tuesday: Frayer Model

Students discuss the word compare using the frayer model as a frame.

Answers vary. For example:

Definition: To look at and discuss 2 or more things.

Example: She has 2 more cookies than he does.

Give a picture example: Students sketch out a comparison with pictures.

Non-example: Add.

Wednesday: Number of the Day

Students write the number 9, draw a picture, put it on the number path and make equations where it is the sum and the difference.

Thursday: Number Talk

Students discuss counting back 3.

Friday: Both Addends Unknown

Students draw the pictures to show the combinations.

Week 34

Monday: Composing Numbers

Answers will vary. Color 4 different ways to make 8. For example: 7 and 1; 6 and 2; 5 and 3.

Tuesday: Draw and Discuss

Answers will vary.

Wednesday: Number Scramble

C.

Thursday: Number Talk

Answers will vary. For example; $10 - 5 = 5$; $9 - 1 = 8$.

Friday: What's the Story?

Stories will vary, example: There are 5 animals. 1 dog and 4 cats.

Week 35

Monday: Composing Numbers

Answers will vary. Color 4 different ways to make 9. For example: 4 and 5; 8 and 1; 6 and 3.

Tuesday: Frayer Model

Students discuss the word square using the frayer model as a frame. Answers vary. For example:

Definition: A 4-sided figure with equal straight sides and angles. It has 4 vertices as well.

Example: A rug; A frame.

Non-Example: A circle.

Picture: (students draw a square).

Wednesday: Number of the Day

14, 10 + 4 = 14, 4 + 10 = 14, fill in the 10 frame, draw 14 circles.

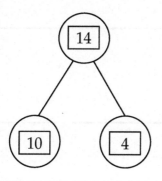

Thursday: Number Strings

9, 8, 7, 6, 5.

Friday: Make Your Own Problem

Answers will vary. For example: The store had 5 rings. It got 2 more. How many does it have now? 7.
Students need to draw a picture.
5 + 2 = 7.

Week 36

Monday: Composing Numbers

Answers will vary. Color 4 different ways to make 10. For example: 9 and 1; 8 and 2; 7 and 3.

Tuesday: Alike and Different

Answers vary; Students discuss the shapes. For example, they both have straight sides. They both have points. They have different sides.

Wednesday: What Doesn't Belong?

6 + 2.

Thursday: Number Talk

Students use fingers, drawings, objects.

Friday: What's the Problem?

Answers vary. For example: 4 − 4; 10 −10.

Week 37

Monday: What Doesn't Belong?

A. 9 is not a teen number.

B. 5 – 3.

Tuesday: It is/It Isn't

It is less than 16; it is not more than 18.

Wednesday: Greater Than, Less Than, in between

Answers will vary.

For example: 1 is less than 2. 15 is greater than 12. 7 is in between 2 and 12.

Thursday: Number Strings

Students look at the idea of taking half away.

Friday: What's the Story?

Answers will vary. There were 10 candies. The kids ate some. Now there are 6 left. How many did they eat?

Week 38

Monday: What Doesn't Belong?

10 – 3; 10 – 6.

Tuesday: Frayer Model

Students discuss teen numbers using the frayer model as a frame.

Answers vary. For example:

Definition: They are the numbers between 11 and 20.

Example: 14.

Non-example: 9.

Sketch: (a base ten sketch or circles).

Wednesday: Number of the Day

19, 19 = 10 + 9, 9 + 10 = 19, One 10 and 9 ones, place in 10 frame, draw 19 circles. The number bond has 19 at the top and then a ten in one circle and a 9 in the other circle.

Thursday: Number Talk

Answers vary.

Friday: Word Problem Sort

The first problem and the answer is 4.

Week 39

Monday: Reasoning Matrix

Carl loves to ice skate, Lucy loves to ride a bike. Sue likes to walk.

Tuesday: Vocabulary

Students discuss 3D shapes using the frayer model as a frame.

Answers vary. For example:

Definition: A 3D shape is not flat. It has faces, edges and vertices.

Example: A cone.

Non-example: A rectangle.

Sketch: Answers vary.

Wednesday: Guess My Number

A. 19.

B. 8.

Thursday: Number Talk

Answers will vary.

Friday: What's the Story?

Stories will vary. For example, I saw 3 turtles and 4 fish. How many animals did I see?

Week 40

Monday: 3 Truths and a Fib
3 is bigger than 7 is false.

Tuesday: Brainstorm

Answers will vary – a ruler, a tape measure, measuring cup.

Wednesday: Number of the Day

Students illustrate 20 in a variety of ways.

Thursday: Number Talk

Answers will vary.

For example: 5 + 5 or 4 – 1.

Friday: What's the Question?

Answers will vary. How many cookies are there altogether?